25 FOODS KIDS HATE

...and how to get them eating 24

25 FOODS KIDS HATE

...and how to get them eating 24

FIONA FAULKNER

This book is dedicated to the three original 'toddler chefs': Darcey, Elsie and Finn. I love all three of you more than I can possibly express. Keep cooking guys!

First published in 2011 by
New Holland Publishers (UK) Ltd
London • Cape Town • Sydney • Auckland
www.newhollandpublishers.com

Garfield House, 86–88 Edgware Road
London W2 2EA, United Kingdom

80 McKenzie Street, Cape Town 8001, South Africa

Unit 1, 66 Gibbes Street, Chatswood NSW 2067, Australia

218 Lake Road, Northcote, Auckland, New Zealand

1 3 5 7 9 10 8 6 4 2

ISBN 978 184773 789 2

Publisher: Clare Sayer
Photography: Ian Garlick
Food stylist: Wendy Sweetser
Design: Lucy Parissi
Production controller: Laurence Poos

Reproduction by Pica Digital PTE Ldt (Singapore)
Printed and bound in Malaysia by Times Offset Bhd Sdn

contents

Introduction 6

The 25 rules every parent should
read before bribing with chocolate 8

How to use this book 16

A note on nutrition 21

THE 25 FOODS: 22

1 Tomatoes 24

2 Carrots and parsnips 28

3 Broccoli 32

4 Peas 36

5 Sweetcorn 40

6 Peppers 44

7 Pumpkin and squash 48

8 Potatoes 52

9 Avocado 56

10 Spinach 60

11 Leeks and greens 64

12 Cauliflower and courgettes 68

13 Slightly sour fruit 72

14 Exotic fruit 76

15 Breakfast 80

16 Slimy foods 84

17 Deli foods 88

18 Herbs, spices and
   stronger flavours 92

19 Meat 96

20 Fish 100

21 Eggs and brown bread 104

22 Rice and grains 108

23 Beans and pulses 112

24 Lentils and legumes 116

25 Going global 120

About the author 124

Index 126

Acknowledgements 128

Introduction

Time and time again I see parents despair that their kids 'fuss with their food' – in particular with vegetables. As they plead with their kids to 'please eat up some more or you won't get dessert,' it's apparent to me that mealtimes are becoming a vicious cycle in which food is the enemy, and the kitchen a battleground.

It was in fact my own story in converting the 'fussy eaters' in my house that first inspired me to set up my business Toddler Chef; my son in particular caused all kinds of mealtime meltdowns. So I know first-hand how emotionally charged and frustrating it can be when the one thing a parent is naturally drawn to do – nurture their offspring with good, wholesome food – is thrown back in their face (yes, sometimes quite literally).

The truth is, while there are many fantastic kids' recipe books out there, most of these are either fairy cake/bakery-driven (nothing wrong with that in itself) or don't tackle the wider issue of fussy eating. It's all very well having a great recipe for a vegetable pasta bake, but what if your kids won't have vegetables on their plate to begin with – or anything that barely resembles 'green food'?

In my own parenting journey I also began to notice that there are very few books out there designed to enable parents and kids to cook together – and this is an integral part of the Toddler Chef ethos. To this end, this isn't just a cookbook; it's a collection of kid-friendly recipes that a parent and child cook together – along with basic cookery techniques for kids to practice and learn. We've become a nation who value speedy-suppers and meals-in-minutes (not to mention designer, pristine kitchens), but I really can't stress enough how vital it is to allow your kids in the kitchen.

Another vital aspect of my Toddler Chef ethos involves the 'PR' skills, games and techniques that I've developed – this is almost where gastronomy meets psychology. It's hugely important to create positive messages around food and these games and techniques underpin everything I do. Think of them as part of your tool kit.

Cookbooks these days often follow a specific theme (speedy, low-fat, vegetarian, Italian etc). In this respect the recipes here may appear to follow no rhyme or reason: some are low-fat, while a few are fried, some are super-simple, others a little more sophisticated, some can be made in less than 60 seconds – one recipe in particular can take up to 3 days to complete. The point I'm making is that my primary concern (or theme) is to simply get your kids excited about good food. To this end I've handpicked the recipes (and tips) that have been the most successful in this objective – with my own kids, and those who come to my workshops – including the fussiest of eaters.

But this book isn't just for fussy eaters – or for toddlers. I hope that parents with kids of every age will find imaginative and inspiring ideas here too. In total I tackle 25 food stuffs (although there are actually over 75 recipes and ideas). I bet your child can be persuaded to enjoy at least 24!

THE 25 RULES

EVERY PARENT SHOULD READ BEFORE BRIBING WITH CHOCOLATE

1. SET ASIDE THE TIME

These days it seems we're cash strapped and time poor – and I'm the first to admit to these challenges of family life. Equally I'm convinced that it's so incredibly vital to set aside small pockets of time to cook with your kids because if you don't teach them (and inspire that love of food), it's doubtful anyone else will. I do worry that the 21st century is creating families who thrive on fast food and ready-meals but are unable to pass down basic cookery skills (or treasured family recipes) to their kids. Don't forget – good eating habits have to be learnt, and therefore taught. Some of the fondest memories I have of my Irish granny are of being perched up on the pub kitchen worktop while she made hearty soups and stews, allowing me to try a few spoonfuls or even stir in some ingredients. Likewise my mum practically weaned me on TV cookery shows when the only celebrity chefs were Delia and Rusty Lee!

2. TAKE A DEEP BREATH – AND GO SHOPPING WITH THE KIDS

Again, I'm not exactly 'on trend' here – and have certainly had my fair share of bored, grumpy kids in shopping trolleys. I'm not suggesting for one minute that you take them on every food shop (and neither am I eschewing online grocery shopping – a godsend for the over-worked, time-stretched parent). But involving your kids in some small way is not only fun for them, it's empowering too. If they can't come shopping, can they help write out (and decide) on the shopping list? Give them choices – 'shall we have carrots or peas with our lasagne tonight?'; attempt to create a sense of discovery and excitement if you are out shopping – 'ooh, this fruit looks unusual – shall we try it?' If you're more of an online (or lone) shopper, you could still involve kids by letting them help you unpack, discussing how and what you can both cook together.

3. GROW YOUR OWN

I'm no Charlie Dimmock (come to that, I'm no Nigella either) but have learnt a few basics along the way. You simply cannot beat the taste and satisfaction of growing and eating your own food – even if this is as simple as a few herb pots on the windowsill. I'll never forget being introduced by my English nan to the joys of finding that first home-grown tomato: the lingering aroma, the warm sweetness… bliss! If you're a complete beginner (as I was, pre-parenting), ask a green-fingered friend to help create a small vegetable patch in your garden, borrow a book from the library or record and watch relevant TV shows.

4. …OR AT LEAST PICK-YOUR-OWN

There's something immensely satisfying about spending a summer's afternoon picking fruit and veg in season – strawberries in particular. Check local papers and notices for details of PYO farms – or simply ask around, especially in villages. I'm all for organic produce – but for me it's just as important to try and eat seasonally and locally. If it's in season, it'll taste great as it hasn't been forcibly grown. If it's local it'll also taste great because it's fresh and won't have travelled for miles on end. Local, seasonal fruit and veg should be fairly easy on the purse strings too. And it just feels good, supporting local farmers. Having said all this, I'm not adverse to buying a gorgeous sweet pineapple or mango from the Caribbean – or to using frozen veg (often frozen veg is packaged very quickly after harvesting, so it retains many important nutrients; frozen peas are a definite staple in our house).

5. GET EAGER ABOUT OMEGAS

I'm pretty evangelical about those so-called 'good fats' and healthy omega oils you may

have read about. They're found in abundance in things such as oily fish, avocados, nuts and seeds. Omega 3 and Omega 6 oils belong to a family of fats known as essential fatty acids. These are vital to our bodies – and have been linked (in some studies) to significantly helping kids with issues such as ADHD, dyspraxia and poor concentration levels at school. On a similar note try and avoid saturated fats and (in particular) any foods with trans-fats.

6. BECOME A MARKETING GURU

While adults generally eat with their taste buds, smell, and emotions, kids eat with their ears, eyes and head. If they don't like the look or sound of something, they probably won't eat it, regardless of how it tastes. Not only this but in my experience it's fair to say that most kids don't especially care whether or not something is good for them. So all your best efforts in imploring them to eat their greens 'because they'll make you big and strong' are probably futile. Young kids in particular have a limited grasp of nutritional values. Kids do care though about how things look – and unfortunately many seem to be hard-wired to hate 'green foods'. With each section in this book, I'll show you how to 'market and PR' those foods in the most effective way possible – from broccoli

here is that kids enjoy something less if they realise they are being rewarded for eating it – i.e. kids ain't stupid! Essentially, if you reward a child with something sweet because they have eaten something they find less palatable, it creates a sense that the sweet food is 'good' and the other is 'bad' (or a punishment) – thus reinforcing the cycle of the child not wanting to eat anything other than the sweet food. This book is all about creating and reinforcing positive messages about food and eating in general.

9. PERSEVERE

Research suggests a child needs to see a new food on average 20 times before they'll want to try it. If they refuse a new food on their plate, don't make a fuss or draw attention to it. If they insist on not having it on their plate, ask if they'd mind 'if mummy or daddy can have it instead?' Ensure you enthusiastically eat it off their plate with a genuine 'ooh thank you, that was delicious!'

trees to potato pillows. And never underestimate the power of using a cookie cutter to create fun sandwiches!

7. RELAX – FUSSINESS IS A NATURAL PHASE

It might help you to know that most kids go through a scientifically proven 'fussy eating stage' (usually somewhere around the 18-month mark). This is thought to be linked to children gravitating towards a sense of independence and their awareness that they are actually able to make choices for themselves – as well as get a reaction from you. Try leaving the room next time they play up with their food – though quietly watch them from a distance to ensure they're safe. It's also thought by some child psychologists that 'fussy eating' is actually a genetic part of human development: a cautious attitude spawned by our prehistoric ancestry when we had to learn what was and wasn't poisonous.

8. NEITHER REWARD NOR PUNISH WITH FOOD

I base this on a very interesting theory called the 'over-justification hypothesis'. The premise

10. OFFER REALISTIC PORTION SIZES

Remember: little tummies only need little portions. Much better to eat one spoonful of peas than none at all. It's sometimes also worth asking the very obvious question: are they actually hungry at the moment? On the subject of size, do also chop vegetables and meat right down to small cubes or chunks – I've found this really does help.

11. WATCH THE SNACK ATTACKS

Parents these days seem obsessed with snacks! Although small children are natural 'grazers' I'd be careful that the snacks you offer are not too filling and are not offered too close to mealtimes. I'd certainly introduce a Last Call for Snacks and preclude kids filling up within 2–3 hours of a main meal. That said, try to be in tune with your child's individual needs. Some kids need heavier snacks (particularly if they're involved in lots of outdoor and physical activities). Another key is to ensure that you always have some fruit or veggie snacks stored

away for when they are hungry. I've found it's far easier to entice them to eat a few veg crudités and dips when they've just come in from school and are genuinely hungry.

12. DON'T FALL INTO THE 'EAT EVERY LAST SCRAP' TRAP

This is particularly important for children who appear to have issues with over-eating or excess weight. By forcing kids to eat 'every last scrap' you are encouraging them to not only over-eat (if they are genuinely not hungry) but also asking them to ignore the vital 'I'm full' signals from their brain. This in turn can lead to over-eating later in life. Equally, try not to let them eat for emotional reasons (such as boredom or sadness). In fact this is an ingrained habit for many of us, and one that I admit I can often struggle with myself.

13. ENCOURAGE 'SILLY SUPPERS'

When your kids are a bit older, create a sense of empowerment (and excitement around food) by enabling them to decide what you'll have for dinner once a week/fortnight/month. Be warned: it may be chips and ice cream all round – but don't fight this. In fact, if the food they choose then makes them feel a little hyperactive, tired or sickly, this is a great lesson learnt. Try not to judge but to encourage self-expression – 'why do you think you felt so hungry or so sick after having all that chocolate for supper?' Use it as an opportunity to discuss how certain foods make us feel if we indulge in too much of them.

14. INVITE FOODIE FRIENDS

This is a tried-and-tested technique. You'd be amazed at what your child will eat when he or she sees their best friend tucking into the same with gusto. Peer pressure at its most effective!

15. EMPLOY THE DISTRACTION TECHNIQUE

Shock-comment alert! I'm a great fan of offering healthy snacks in front of a kids' favourite TV show (it's the 'hand-to-mouth' action). If you can get them eating healthy snacks in front of a TV cookery show, that's a double-whammy! I've found that my obsession with foodie shows has gone a long way in inspiring my kids to eat – Darcey's current favourite is the Barefoot Contessa! Equally this works on long, arduous car journeys (obviously watch for choking hazards, particularly with small kids). This technique always did the trick

with Elsie, my younger daughter, who'd refuse carrots on her plate but happily much away on one in the car, staring out of the window.

16. BE PATIENT – AND DON'T PANIC

One of the things I tell parents who come to my Toddler Chef workshops is that good eating habits take time. Some kids take to new ideas immediately; others can take weeks before they even consider trying anything new. Kids won't actually allow themselves to starve to death – and it's extremely doubtful they'll become malnourished either. If you're seriously concerned about your child's eating habits, do consult your GP.

17. CHANGE THE SCENERY

This is another 'marketing' technique from Toddler Chef HQ. Have a tea party in your child's playhouse, a lunch picnic in the garden or even supper on a rug in the lounge. Shake up the routine a bit, stick on a CD and make it fun by allowing teddy or their favourite toy to join in too.

18. WATCH THE LOW-FAT AND LOW-SUGAR ALTERNATIVES

While I agree that too much fat and sugar is a bad thing, I'd far rather see sugar than an artificial sweetener. Check the ingredients and research these chemicals – because that's exactly what they are. So-called 'juice drinks' and cordials can be real 'chemical culprits'. Remember: while sugar and other fats can be burnt off with exercise, chemicals stay in your child's bloodstream and have been linked to hyperactivity amongst other things. Go online, do your research and make up your own mind.

19. ...BUT DON'T BECOME THE PARTY BAG EQUIVALENT TO THE SPANISH INQUISITION!

On the other hand, it's rare to find a children's birthday party gift bag without a stash of chewy sweets laden with all manner of chemicals and additives. I relax the rules on party bags as I don't want anything to become the coveted 'forbidden fruit'. And to be honest, I secretly love the odd sweetie myself.

reasonably good kids' menus and table activities) and don't have unrealistic expectations of very young children. If you don't all sit together as a family to eat at home, your child won't be at all used to doing this at a restaurant. As with good eating habits, good table manners must be learnt and therefore taught – and once again, these start at home.

21. THINK ABOUT YOUR CHILD'S PERSONALITY

Interestingly, some research suggests that kids who are particularly sensitive to new surroundings, textures, or even loud noise can be particularly reticent to try new foods. Consider the role your child's personality has to play – including with some of the games and techniques I suggest.

22. IF THEY WON'T EAT 'EM, JUICE 'EM!

I cannot stress enough how often we use the juicer in our house. I promise you that getting clever with juice can totally revolutionize your kids' fruit and veg intake. Never mind 5 a day – clever juicing can fast-track you up to 10 a day – imagine that! Don't confuse a juicer with a blender or smoothie maker – and remember that fresh juice is very different from juice bought in a carton simply because the latter is always heat-treated (which kills off stacks of the nutrients). My carrot and apple combo is consistently a winner (see page 28).

23. KEEP A DIARY

It's very easy to think that progress has been slim. Ensure you note down all the little successes – no matter how small they seem – and keep a note of what does and doesn't seem to work for your child. Try and scrapbook recipe ideas too.

24. EQUIP YOURSELF

There are plenty of miniature versions of cookery equipment for kids – from mini whisks and rolling pins through to chef's hats and aprons. Having their own 'cooks kit' can make kids feel so much more involved. If money is

20. TAKE THEM OUT

This tip works on two levels: firstly, get them out and about in the fresh air (nothing better to build up an appetite). Secondly, and if budgets allow, take them to a restaurant now and again. There's nothing more rewarding than being able to take your child to a restaurant in the knowledge that they know what's expected of them and how to behave. Pick and choose venues wisely (many chains now have

tight, create a 'wish list' for when friends and relatives ask what they'd like for birthdays or Christmas. Equally, do ensure you have a few basics of your own (see Equipment, page 18).

25. SET AN EXAMPLE

Ok, I do mention this a lot – but without doubt it's worth repeating again and again as its one of my most important pieces of advice I can give: the more good foods your kids see you eat, the more likely they are to imitate your behaviour. One of my favourite techniques here is to eat something next to your kids, watch their natural curiosity take over, and then pretend to begrudgingly allow them to graze from your plate. Slightly unorthodox (and some would say encourages bad-manners) but it's actually a very effective technique when you can later remind them at their own mealtime that 'you do like mushrooms actually – remember you ate some of mummy's yesterday..?' In an ideal world though we'd all be eating the same meals (kids and adults). I know this can be unrealistic but it would be really helpful if you ate at least some of what you expect your kids to eat. Perhaps you might like some of the recipes here!

How to use this book

Obviously you could easily dip in and out of the recipes in this book or read the whole thing from cover to cover. Either way, I've tried to make it easy and informative for you – for example look out for the ✹ icon. One splat suggests a reasonably mess-free recipe; three splats indicate that you might not want to wear your favourite designer blouse!

I also wanted to highlight where recipes assist in developing physical dexterity and help kids learn special cookery skills – so look out for the heads-up I give on these too. In fact I'm a firm believer that cooking with kids develops so much more than conventional cookery techniques – you can transfer skills from pretty much the entire school curriculum: geography – 'where does this dish come from?'; languages – 'what is this dish in French/Spanish?'; numeracy – 'let's count the tomatoes/weigh the flour'... I could go on.

The other thing I've done with my recipes is to include 'gourmet for grown-ups' footnotes. Essentially this is to inspire you to create the dishes not just for the kids, but for all of you. I'd love it if you enjoyed these dishes as much as your kids did. After all, who wants to cook three or four different meals every night?

I did wonder whether to single out certain recipes for certain age groups – but the truth is, all the recipes in this book can involve all kids to a greater or lesser degree (from about 18 months to teens – including those with special needs or learning difficulties). I give you prompts and ideas rather than prescriptive steps simply because you know your child(ren) better than anyone – their likes and dislikes and what they're capable of, plus their boredom threshold. Even if some recipes are lower-key than others (in terms of what they can help with) consider letting kids weigh and prepare the ingredients – or even just let them watch as you undertake more complex tasks (or the jobs over the hob that you feel they're too young for). A good rule of thumb is simply to keep them occupied – and engaged in what they're doing.

KNIFE SKILLS

I must also add that I do allow my eldest, Darcey (who is now 7), to cut certain foods with a proper sharp knife (mushrooms, green beans etc.) – although always with me (sometimes anxiously) watching her. For obvious reasons I don't undertake this practice with kids who are not my own. But I do believe that if a child is old enough – and understands the responsibility of using sharp implements – and if you guide them and keep them safe (always cut vegetables that are sitting flatly on a surface – i.e. not able to roll around), then knife skills can be learnt at a reasonably young age. If you're not sure, perhaps start your child off with a vegetable peeler and see how they get on. If you do allow your child to use a knife, be sure to tell them to take their time and relax. Teach them how to hold and carry them safely. This may feel counter-intuitive but sharp knives that cut quickly and effectively are actually

safer than blunt ones. Try and encourage your kids to use the 'claw hand' technique with the non-chopping hand (i.e. fingers tucked in) and wear closed-toe shoes (just in case). Challenge your child in their cooking – and yourself in what you're prepared to let them have a go at.

SAFETY

Having said all of the above on letting your child 'have a go' – the most important thing of all is staying safe. Don't let kids too close to open flames, hot rings on the hob, boiling water (or oil) or sharp knives when unattended/too young. Please don't ever leave any child alone in the kitchen cooking or preparing food.

Needless to say you also need to employ basic hygiene standards (washing hands before you cook, using different boards for raw meat and other foods, keeping everything at the right temperature).

EQUIPMENT

There's nothing more annoying that starting a recipe and then realizing that you don't have all the right gear – so I do let you know within each recipe where you will need a particular bit of kit. To be honest, as lovely as it is to have half the Lakeland catalogue, you can get away with surprisingly little. But if you're serious about home cooking, you will need a few bits and bobs. I'm not saying spend a fortune – and if you can, borrow stuff off friends and family or again, chuck things on your Christmas list – but these are the things that I wouldn't be without and that many of my recipes actually do need to complete:

• A food processor that can finely chop up vegetables. If it's a big expensive one that comes with a blender as standard, fantastic. If not, you'll need a…

• …blender/liquidiser. This could be a freestanding machine or a hand-held blender. So-called 'smoothie makers' do pretty much the same job.

A FEW FINAL WORDS

Read up! A good cook's tip is to first read the recipe from beginning to end – preferably when the kids aren't around and you can concentrate. It just makes it easier if you have an idea of what's coming next, what the kids can do, and the equipment you might need.

Watch the labels I mention the phrase 'fussy eaters' a lot when in conversation with parents (and in this book). But I'm also very careful not to mention this phrase in front of kids, or label them as a 'fussy eater' or 'difficult with food' – and I encourage parents to do the same. Not only may kids revert to type and simply live up to this expectation but it also embraces a culture of blame and negativity – that there's something wrong with the child. Instead, I'd encourage you to stay positive around the idea of food and eating (I know it's hard sometimes – I really have been soooooo frustrated in the past). In any case, shouldn't we all be a bit fussy with our food? I openly reject unripe peaches, bland tomatoes and fatty meat.

Don't worry! I know I've already stated this but let me reassure you again. Many, many children go through a fussy eating stage and the vast majority do grow out of it. This book is designed to both reassure and help you along the way. I can't promise that it will magically transform your child's eating habits – but I'm certain that what I've learnt along the way in my own journey will at least help – and, I hope, will inspire you too. Do let me know how you get on via the Toddler Chef website (www.toddlerchef. com). I read every email and would love to hear your story.

APRONS ON? LET'S COOK...!

The next two aren't absolutely essential – but I just wouldn't be without them:
• A stand mixer (with whisk attachment and dough hook) – for baking/pizza dough making.
• A juicer – most are really simple to use and dishwasher proof. Buy the best juicer that your budget will allow – preferably one with a wide enough chute so you don't have to chop anything up – and don't let it sit there in a box under the bed! I also love my:
• ...microplane grater, ice-cream scoop (for decanting perfect amounts of cake mix into cupcake cases – top tip!), and kitchen scissors – why chop when you can cut?

A note on nutrition

I'm not a nutritionist but do have a healthy interest in food that will nourish kids and boost their immune systems. Any nutritional notes in this book are simply the result of my own reading and 'borrowed' information really that I've picked up along the way.

With this in mind, I've tried to limit the amount of salt I use (in keeping with national guidelines). That said, as you'll see, I'm not afraid to use salt where I feel a recipe benefits from a little seasoning. But do try and be aware of using excess salt (in all your diets). Where I stipulate use of stock, think about using a low-salt stock for example – or of course make your own.

When it comes to sugar and fats, while I'm mindful of the childhood obesity problem we have in western society, this book is not purposefully designed to cut back on fats and sugars. Some dishes are lower in fat than others (though most, I think, would be described as either very or reasonably healthy). My view is, everything in moderation and exercise, exercise, exercise! Sugars and fats can be burnt off so while I don't feel that either of these should be consumed excessively, I do feel that as long as your child isn't clinically overweight and as long as they're getting a decent amount of exercise (and brushing their teeth) you needn't worry about the odd treat or two. If however your child is struggling to keep their weight down, consult your GP.

A quick note on dried fruit – I know a lot of parents use this as a 'healthy snack.' To be honest, I'm not the biggest fan of dried fruit; my slight aversion to it goes deeper than personal taste. Many dentists are now showing concern that these sticky, sugary little treats (and yes, they're full of sugar, albeit fruit sugar) are seriously eroding our kids' teeth. I'm no dental expert – head online and search around a bit for the dentistry viewpoint on fruit sugars – but it makes sense that something so sticky and sugary is harder to remove by brushing teeth alone. I don't mean to scaremonger and I appreciate that many dried fruits have vitamin and mineral attributes – such as the iron in dried apricots – so perhaps just go easy and bear these words in mind.

THE25FOODS

tomatoes

MARKETING TOMATOES

I always start each new Toddler Chef term with tomatoes so it made sense to showcase them here as the first food in the book. Truth be told, I think there's no better way to eat tomatoes than simply as they are – preferably home-grown, in season and *never* from the fridge (it kills the taste and lovely warm, oozy middle). I've had a drip-feed success effect with my son Finn by simply leaving cherry tomatoes out on the fruit bowl with the other fruit, letting him pick one up as he wanders by – and ensuring he sees me do the same – that's my first tip.

There's a world of difference between the tomatoes we buy in the shops and what we can grow in our gardens and I'm a complete home-grown evangelist. Home-grown tomatoes are succulent, juicy and so, so sweet. And that smell – it's one of my favourite smells in the world. Did you know that the smell itself is derived from the green stem? In fact, some professional chefs finely chop the stem and add it to tomato sauces in order to allow that tomato muskiness to pervade and enhance.

Failing that, buy the best you can. I'm not one to suggest that parents should buy *everything* organic and top-end but really, if there's one thing I feel you should splash out on, it's tomatoes.

TRY THIS...

The game that's always been as popular with parents as with kids is the Tom Tom Tomato Game, using the fantastic children's song, *Tom Tom Tomato*. The game encourages kids to use tomatoes in a variety of different ways – without having to eat them until they're ready to. You don't have to use the song (although it provides a nice little intro to the game as well as a positive message). It aims to appeal to your child's mischievous spirit. It also gives them choices – and kids love being given choices.

> **❝***God bless the Tommy Tomato song; it's now legendary in our house!***❞**
> **Natasha and Clive Howard, parents to Chloe (aged 5)**

So, play the song (or not) – and allow your child(ren) to pick out their 'favourite tomato' from a bowl. Some kids won't want to touch a tomato at this stage. That's fine. You play the game and let them watch. If you're playing the song, at the point that you hear the lyric 'Tom tom tomato pops inside...' tell your child that they have 'three choices' as to what they want to do with their tomato:

- They can give it a little kiss
- They can pretend its lipstick / warrior war paint and put it over their lips / face!
- They can squirt it in their mouth and make a 'squelch' noise!

Don't look disappointed if they refuse to eat it. Ensure you eat your own tomato and perhaps theirs too. This game works really well in groups – especially with other kids who love tomatoes.

Tom Tom Tomato published by CYP Music – available from www.kidsmusic.co.uk.

CHEESY TOMATO CRUMBLE

This dish is intensely 'tomatoey' although the cheese crust in the crumble does balance it out. I use a little sugar to enhance the natural sweetness of a tomato. If you really want to 'superfood' this recipe, you could add a handful of seeds to the crumble mix (sunflower or a handful of sesame).

COOKERY SKILLS: I CAN LEARN HOW TO RUB BUTTER INTO FLOUR TO MAKE A CRUMBLE

SHOPPING LIST

3 medium-large tomatoes, roughly chopped.

2 tbsp olive oil

½ tsp sugar

1 garlic clove, crushed

2 pinches of salt

50 g (2 oz) plain flour

50 g (2 oz) unsalted butter – not too hard, not too soft

50 g (2 oz) oats

25 g (1 oz) grated Italian cheese

25 g (1 oz) flaked almonds

SERVES 4
(2 ADULTS, 2 KIDS)

APRONS ON, LET'S COOK!

1 Preheat the oven to 190°C/375°F/gas 5.

2 Here's where things might get messy! In a large bowl, and using your hands, combine the tomatoes with the oil. Here's where your child can really get stuck in and enjoy handling tomatoes. Admittedly, it could be done with a metal spoon – but I think it's nice to get kids actually handling the tomatoes.

3 Add the sugar, garlic and a good pinch of salt and stir through with a spoon. Your child can help here too. Place into an ovenproof dish.

4 To make the crumble – and again, we're gonna get messy – place the flour and another good pinch of salt in a mixing bowl and add the butter. With your hands, rub the butter into the flour until it resembles breadcrumbs (this is another great job for kids to do).

5 Stir through the oats, grated cheese and flaked almonds.

6 Put the oaty crumble mixture on top of the tomatoes. Place in the preheated oven and bake for about 35 minutes or until the topping is cooked through, crispy and golden. Watch out: the tomatoes take a while to cool down.

GOURMET FOR GROWN-UPS

Garnish and serve with fresh basil. Add chopped hazelnuts or a little mustard powder to the crumble or good-quality cooked ham to the tomatoes. Serve with a jug of hot cheese sauce – this could be a hit at the lunch table on a cold wintry day.

DARCEY'S INSIDE-OUT TOMATO SANDWICHES

This has bread and butter on the inside and tomato on the outside! My older daughter Darcey always asks for these. If you want, although it can be fiddly, start off with baby tomatoes – just make sure they are juicy and sweet.

COOKERY SKILLS: I CAN LEARN HOW TO CAREFULLY SPOON MIXTURES INTO VEGETABLES

APRONS ON, LET'S COOK!

1 Preheat the oven to 200°C/400°F/gas 6 and lightly grease a baking tray.

2 Slice the top from each tomato. With a teaspoon, carefully scoop out the flesh of four of the tomatoes – perhaps a child can help here. Place it in a bowl, setting aside the hollows. Scoop out the flesh of the other two but don't add this to the bowl – we don't need it for this dish so feel free to eat it, but add the hollowed out tomatoes to the baking tray. Chop up all this tomato flesh with a knife and fork – then ask a child to stir it up.

3 Melt the butter in a small non-stick frying pan. Add the breadcrumbs and sauté over a medium heat for 3 minutes until warm and crispy.

4 Add the breadcrumbs, cheese and pesto to the chopped tomato flesh and mix well. Carefully fill the six tomato hollows with this stuffing mixture – again, this is a perfect opportunity for a child to help.

5 With all the stuffed tomatoes on the greased baking tray, bake in the preheated oven for about 8 minutes.

GOURMET FOR GROWN-UPS

Try using bigger 'beef' tomatoes. I also like to add chopped sun-dried tomatoes and top with a ring of goats' cheese, serving with a sprig of fresh basil in the middle and perhaps a single black olive just next to it. You could use this as an attractive side dish at a dinner party.

carrots and parsnips

MARKETING CARROTS AND PARSNIPS

If your child struggles to have either carrots or parsnips on their plate, try buying a few (still with their green stems in tact) and use as part of an art and craft activity. Buy stickers for eyes, draw on noses and mouths and supervise kids as they trim the green 'hair'. In this way, as your child becomes comfortable with handling them, they are more likely to be happy having them on their plate.

TRY THIS...

I love carrots. Although I must confess to preferring them raw to cooked – and I think a lot of people feel the same way. My absolute favourite way of eating carrots though is to *drink* them and I've had huge success with kids and carrots in this way. Buy a juicer, bung in two carrots and two apples. That's it. Or try freshly squeezed carrot and orange juice. If your child refuses this, how about you create little 'ice cubes' out of it and add to their favourite drink?

Try raw grated carrot in sandwiches – it works really well with hummus (as well as with cream cheese).

Parsnips are a bit of a 'love 'em or hate 'em' food and are from the same family as carrots. Try roasting them with olive oil, garlic and a dash of honey for the last 10 minutes or so of the cooking time.

Feel free to also use parsnips in the carrot recipe here, and vice versa.

"Just wanted to say thank you – today my son had carrot for the first time!**"**

Joanne Lulham, mum to Carter (aged 2)

PARSNIP RISOTTO

Parsnip risotto?! Yes, really – and it's utterly delicious too (plus a great first introduction to rice). The trick here is to ensure that you dice the parsnips into the smallest cubes you can. You don't have to serve it with the parsnip crisps – but I do think they give the dish an added dimension.

COOKERY SKILLS: I CAN PRACTISE STIRRING SLOWLY AND SAFELY

SHOPPING LIST

2 large parsnips, peeled and woody stems removed

35 g (1½ oz) unsalted butter

2 tbsp olive oil

1 onion, finely chopped

185 g (6½ oz) risotto rice (I tend to use Arborio, but ensure it hasn't been pre-flavoured)

600 ml (1 pint) hot vegetable stock

25 g (1 oz) grated Parmesan

Salt

SERVES 2-4

APRONS ON, LET'S COOK!

1 Finely dice one of the parsnips for the risotto and use a mandolin or vegetable peeler to create fine shavings from the other for the crisps.

2 Use a large non-stick saucepan or frying pan and melt the butter and 1 tablespoon of oil over a medium–high heat. Add the onion and sauté for a couple of minutes.

3 Now add the diced parsnip and sauté for about 5 minutes until they're softer and slightly smaller. Don't have the heat too high – you can't rush risotto!

4 Next add the rice and keep stirring it in the pan for a minute or two. It will immediately absorb the butter and oil and the mix will feel drier. This may be a good point for an older child to help out and have a stir.

5 Now it's time to s-l-o-w-l-y add the stock. Simply pour in small amounts and keep stirring until the stock is fully absorbed. Then add another little bit. Keep going – you'll probably use most of it – until it's all absorbed and the rice is tender and the mix is just a little bit sticky. This will take at least 20 minutes – again, don't have the heat too high. Let your child safely have a stir or two.

6 While this is going on, take a small frying pan and heat up about 1 tbsp olive oil. Add a pinch of salt too. Once it's hot fry the parsnip shavings for 4–5 minutes until golden brown, turning with a spatula or tongs. Transfer to a plate with some kitchen towel to absorb any excess oil.

7 Once you're happy with the risotto, take it off the heat and immediately stir through the parmesan. If it then feels too dry or sticky, add a touch more stock to loosen it slightly.

8 Serve with the parsnip crisps on top (cut up if necessary).

GOURMET FOR GROWN-UPS

Create little arancini 'balls' from the risotto and serve with a rich tomato-based sauce and some fresh rocket leaves. The perfect light lunch – just add sunshine, a glass of chilled white, and your best girlfriends!

GOURMET FOR GROWN-UPS

Double the amount of sage leaves and reserve some back to use as a garnish. Add a bit of seasoning after you blitz (and maybe some extra stock) and serve this as a soup with a swirl of crème fraîche, a sprinkling of toasted pine nuts and a few sage leaves.

ORANGE SPAGHETTI

I must confess, this is one of my favourite recipes – and it does have a pretty good success rate. Here are a few tips: while you're organising your ingredients, have the carrots left out and ask your child to arrange them in order of size, smallest first. When they're bored of that, get them to count out the sage leaves for you, 1–10. Encourage them to smell the sage – and talk about their lovely dark green colour. You'll need a food processor for this recipe.

COOKERY SKILLS: I CAN COUNT OUT CARROTS – AND SOFT LEAFY HERBS

SHOPPING LIST

500 g (1 lb) carrots

50 g (2 oz) unsalted butter

About 10 fresh sage leaves

3 shallots, chopped into small pieces (or a finely chopped small–medium onion)

400 ml (14 fl oz) hot vegetable stock

25 g (1 oz) pine nuts (optional)

Enough fresh or dried spaghetti for a family of four

Grated Parmesan, to serve

**SERVES 4
(2 ADULTS, 2 KIDS)**

APRONS ON, LET'S COOK!

1 Peel the carrots and slice them into small discs. As you do so, throw them into a nearby bowl. You could make it into a fun game – 'hey, do you think I'll be able to get this one into the bowl, or will I miss?!' Any that land outside the bowl can be yours to eat ('mmm, that one's mine!'). Offer one to your child. Oh, and don't eat too many – we need them for the recipe!

2 Melt the butter in a large non-stick saucepan over a medium heat. As it starts to get very hot and frothy, carefully add the sage leaves (if your child is still watching, you could count them in together). Gently fry the sage leaves until they go a bit crispy (about 2 minutes). Then, very carefully, remove them and set aside.

3 Just as carefully, add the shallots or onion to the same pan – still over a medium heat – and sauté for 1–2 minutes. The butter may be a bit brown in places but don't worry. Add the carrots and stir-fry for about 2 minutes until everything is mixed through.

4 Now add half of the stock. Everything will come up to an immediate simmer. Over a low–medium heat let it all simmer for about 15–20 minutes, stirring from time-to-time. Basically you want the carrots to soften and absorb all (or most) of the stock. After 10 minutes or so, you might want to think about cooking up some spaghetti.

5 Once the carrots are cooked and most of the stock absorbed, leave it all to cool slightly. Then add the reserved sage leaves and stir through. Next blitz it all up in your blender or food processor. Your kids may like to see this in motion – but do warn them it will be noisy. Use as much (or all) of the remaining stock in order to create a sauce-like consistency that you know your kids will like.

6 Stir through the pine nuts and you're done! Simply use as you would any other pasta sauce. My kids love it with a sprinkling of grated Parmesan cheese. I think this, along with the pine nuts, make it feel like an orange 'pasta pesto'.

broccoli

MARKETING BROCCOLI

I do think that one of the key points with marketing broccoli is to cut off tiny small stems – much more appealing for kids and less of a hurdle for you in trying to get them to eat huge quantities. The concept of 'broccoli trees' was one I'd heard of years before I set up Toddler Chef, so I can hardly claim the idea as my own, but it's certainly one of the most-used PR exercises both at home and in my classes and workshops. I do take it one step further though and try and refer to them as baby broccoli trees – cooking the smallest stems possible, then (once a child is happy to eat broccoli) we move on to Daddy Broccoli, Mummy Broccoli and Baby Broccoli (according to their size).

TRY THIS...

I'm not a huge fan of hiding puréed vegetables in sauces and feel this defeats the object of getting your child to love the taste and texture of a variety of veg. Sometimes though, puréeing fruit and vegetables does work for certain recipes without disguising their taste or colour (such as the red repper sauce on page 46). Also, it can sometimes just help to maintain a parent's peace of mind, knowing that their kids have had at least some veg for dinner.

If your child will absolutely not eat broccoli, I think puréeing it and hiding it could be appropriate here. This is simply because broccoli is just so darn healthy – a bona fide superfood and one that I'm pretty obsessed with getting everyone eating more of. If you do hide broccoli in sauces and soups, continue presenting it in its whole form too, just to encourage your child to eat it like this.

> **❝**What I love about Fiona is how she reminded us of the simplicity of some ingredients. Once my daughter had torn up those baby broccoli trees, she was more than happy to watch me cook them – and then eat them herself!**❞**
>
> **Jill Wren, mum to Sophia (aged 4)**

BABY BROCCOLI PASTA

It took me years to discover the joy of stir-fried broccoli and it's now probably my favourite way to eat it. This recipe really plays on the concept of broccoli being 'little green trees' – and stir-frying your little trees in this way gives them brilliant crunch and a gorgeous vibrant colour. The sesame seeds give added texture (and all those sneaky omega oils) and the pesto just carries the whole thing – continuing with the positive messages around 'green food.' If you really want to super-charge it, add in some flaked salmon too. Don't be tempted to just bung in bigger bits of broccoli – the smaller 'trees' do make the difference.

COOKERY SKILLS: I CAN CREATE BABY BROCCOLI TREES WITH MY HANDS

SHOPPING LIST

Enough dried pasta for a family of four

4 large broccoli florets

1 x 190 g (7 oz) jar of green pesto

15 g (½ oz) butter

Small handful sesame seeds

SERVES 4
(2 ADULTS, 2 KIDS)

APRONS ON, LET'S COOK!

1 Bring a large pan of water to the boil and cook the pasta until just al dente. I use fusilli (twirls) a lot for this pasta dish.

2 Meanwhile, using your hands, break the broccoli florets right down into tiny 'baby trees' – obviously this is a great job for kids to get involved with. Don't worry if the trees break a bit or it gets messy. If there aren't any kids around, kitchen scissors will do a quicker job of this (or for the bulk of this job).

3 Melt the butter in a large pan and stir-fry the broccoli over a medium–high heat for about 3 minutes.

4 Drain the cooked pasta, return to the pan and tip in the green pesto sauce, stirring it through. Add the broccoli trees and then ask a child to sprinkle over the sesame seeds.

GOURMET FOR GROWN-UPS

The only real tweak I add to this – though it does make a big difference in flavour – is topping it with lots of fresh coriander. I could eat platefuls of this!

BROCCOLI BAKED POTATOES

I think it was (the wonderful) food writer Nigel Slater who once said that baked potatoes are the culinary equivalent of a hug. I couldn't agree more – and this is a lunchtime favourite for me as well as my children. There's absolutely no shame in using frozen broccoli here (I tend to buy as much frozen as fresh) – you'll just have to cook it that little bit longer. You'll need a blender or food processor for this recipe.

COOKERY SKILLS: I CAN LEARN HOW TO MASH POTATO

SHOPPING LIST

1 baking potato

About 50 g (2 oz) broccoli (fresh or frozen)

A dash of olive oil

25 g (1 oz) grated Swiss cheese

2 tbsp milk

A knob of unsalted butter

½ tsp Dijon mustard

25 g (1 oz) cream cheese

Salt and pepper

SERVES 1

APRONS ON, LET'S COOK!

1 Preheat the oven to 200°C/400°F/gas 6.

2 Prick the potato with a fork. Put the oil and a pinch of salt in a dish and coat the potato all over. This will give it a deliciously crisp, golden skin. Perhaps get your child to oil the potatoes, and then you can do the salt.

3 Put the potato directly on the oven shelf and bake for about 45 minutes, or until you know the flesh is cooked through.

4 After about 30 minutes, steam or lightly boil the broccoli until it is cooked but still with some crunch – this should take about 8–10 minutes.

5 Once the spuds are cooked, remove (carefully with kitchen gloves) from the oven and leave to cool for about 10 minutes. Keep the oven on.

6 While you're waiting for the potato to cool a bit, whizz up the broccoli in a blender or food processor.

7 With a sharp knife, cut across the top quarter of the potato. Carefully scoop out the inner flesh – trying not to tear the outer 'jacket' – and place it all in a bowl. Add the cheese, butter and milk to the potato in the bowl and mash it all up thoroughly. This could be a good job for a kid to help with.

8 Stir through the blended broccoli, cream cheese and Dijon mustard – again, get the kids involved. Add some seasoning and taste the mash – does it need more of anything? Be quite relaxed about the fact that there's broccoli in there. Don't draw attention to it needlessly.

9 Now both of you can spoon the mash back into the hollow skin. Pile it up a bit, although you'll still have a bit more than you'll need. Place the filled potato back in the oven for another 10 minutes or so.

10 You could decorate the baked potato once it's ready: 2 olives for eyes; half a cherry tomato for a nose; or chopped chives to create 'green grass' for an artistic garden scene.

peas

MARKETING PEAS

Peas fall under that very tricky banner of 'green food' (oh no!), so you may have to 'PR' them a bit. Have you ever noticed that they're a very popular side dish with lots of Children's Menus at pubs and cafés? Come to that, have you ever got into an argument with your kid to 'eat some more peas!' It's not worth it. If they have a spoonful and enjoy them, that must be better than a forced plateful that they will resent.

In terms of marketing peas, why not give your child lots of choices: fresh peas from the pod (see below), hot peas that have been boiled up for a bit, with or without butter and mint, mushy peas with chips. Ask them 'which do you prefer?'

TRY THIS...

I love peas! In fact, they're probably my favourite vegetable. Though frozen peas are a staple in our house, there's something very special about eating peas from the pod, while in season. Try grabbing a handful of pea pods next time you have a long car journey coming up and offering as a car snack, letting your child crack open the pods and pick at the sweet green 'treasure' inside.

I often play the Green Pea Passenger Train at my Toddler Chef workshops at the end when we do Story Time. I hand out pea pods and invite kids to open them and count up how many green pea passengers they've found inside, riding in the 'train'. Then, while I'm reading, they're invited to eat these as a story-time snack.

> ❝We started Toddler Chef as my daughter Annalise is a very cautious eater, she will not eat anything she does not trust. Toddler Chef has worked wonders for her confidence with food. I can't tell you what an achievement it felt when she licked a tomato or tried peas (and then proceeded to eat a cup full!)❞
>
> **Stephanie Lewis, mum to Annalise (aged 4)**

PEA AND CRANBERRY CROSTINI

This is the kind of dish that you could easily modify to suit your child's taste buds. The end result as it stands could (arguably) do with some seasoning. This is good example of where what works for an adult's palate may not work for a kid's – sometimes kids just prefer less dramatic flavours. Feel free to tweak it. It's a great idea to sell this dish to your children as 'Green and Red Jewelled Flying Saucers' to make it more fun and appealing.

COOKERY SKILLS: I CAN LEARN HOW TO MASH VEGETABLES AND USE A PASTRY BRUSH

SHOPPING LIST

1 French bread baguette

A glug of olive oil

1 tsp unsalted butter

50 g (2 oz) frozen peas

40 g (1½ oz) goats' cheese or ricotta

15 g (½ oz) dried cranberries

MAKES 3

APRONS ON, LET'S COOK!

1 Slice three little rounds of bread reasonably thickly so that you have three circular shapes.

2 Brush these with a little oil (maybe a little person could help here) and place under a hot grill for a short while until the bread just crisps up a bit (don't let it toast).

3 Melt the butter in a saucepan and add the peas. Cook them until they've still got a bit of crunch and flavour, stirring as you go (it shouldn't take more than 3–5 minutes).

4 Take the pan off the heat and mash the peas down a bit. Add the goats' cheese or ricotta and cranberries and give everything a good stir. If the pan's not too hot, maybe a child could help.

5 Spoon equally over the crisped bread and serve immediately.

GOURMET FOR GROWN-UPS

I'd definitely add some seasoning – a sprinkling of sea salt and a good twist of black pepper. In fact if I make these as grown-up canapés I tend to slice the bread thinner, stick with the goats' cheese (I'm not the biggest fan of ricotta but my kids seem to like it) and reduce the amount of cranberries slightly.

EMILY'S PEA AND LIME DIP

This dish will always have a special place in my heart because I've used it so much at so many workshops and road shows. My friend Katie's daughter (Emily) says it's her favourite recipe from a workshop she once did, aged 8. You will need a blender or food processor for this recipe and you'll also need to plan ahead by defrosting some frozen peas.

COOKERY SKILLS: I CAN LEARN TO MEASURE OUT INGREDIENTS

SHOPPING LIST

100 g (3½ oz) frozen peas, defrosted (but still cold and firm)

75 g (3 oz) cream cheese (low-fat if you prefer)

15 g (½ oz) grated parmesan cheese

1 tsp fresh lime juice

SERVES 3–4 HUNGRY KIDS AS A SNACK

APRONS ON, LET'S COOK!

There are two ways of preparing this dip:

1 The quick and easy way is to shove everything into a blender or food processor and blitz. Ta-da!

2 OR – and I have done this on a few occasions – you can get a child to measure everything out, put it in a bowl and mix, then 'scrunch' it all together with their (clean) hands. Works just as well – and you can get them to lick their fingers afterwards – but boy is it messy.

3 Serve with vegetable crudités or my tortilla chips (see page 93).

GOURMET FOR GROWN-UPS

To hike the dip up a notch, add in some fresh mint (torn), more lime juice, seasoning and perhaps some finely sliced spring onions. Serve topped with grated lime zest.

sweetcorn

MARKETING SWEETCORN

One of my favourite Toddler Chef ways to market sweetcorn is to use a game. Leave out a little bowl in the centre of a table and invite kids to take one single kernel (call them 'sweetie sweetcorns' or something similar). Tell them to place it in their mouth and I have to go round the room and guess where a child has 'hidden' their sweetie sweetcorn: under their tongue; over their tongue; in their cheek etc? This can cause huge merriment for kids who like to out-do me or trick members of the group. Having said all this, it's worth me pointing out (for the record) that there are some foods that kids will naturally just never like – and my daughter Darcey absolutely and resolutely hates sweetcorn. You win some, you lose some…

TRY THIS…

It seems to have gone out of fashion to eat corn-on-the-cob but actually this is a lovely way of introducing kids to sweetcorn – and it's an instant hand-held snack! I found a lovely recipe recently that marinated corn-on-the-cob with a little butter, sugar and desiccated coconut. Sweetcorn on pizza is also a good idea. Or, next time you make pancakes, try adding a handful of sweetcorn and a little soft brown sugar to the batter.

CREAMY CORN CHOWDER

This is an all-time favourite of mine – and a lot of kids I know happen to love it too (well except Darcey with her categorical aversion to the small yellow things). The semolina adds backbone and texture, the sweet potato adds sweetness and the sage plays a supporting role with additional flavour. If I'm making this for adults, I always add a little kick too (see below). Kids who like – and are used to – spicy food may cope with the same but I wouldn't risk it on the first attempt. Garlic bread is a particularly good food buddy here. And by the way, you'll need a blender or food processor for this recipe.

COOKERY SKILLS: I CAN PRACTISE PEELING POTATOES

SHOPPING LIST

400 g (13 oz) sweet potato (about 2), peeled and cubed

25 g (1 oz) butter

2 tbsp olive oil

1 onion, finely chopped

500 ml (17 fl oz) hot vegetable stock

600 g (1 lb 5 oz) drained weight tinned sweetcorn (no sugar or salt added) – or fresh/frozen

150 ml (¼ pint) single cream

25 g (1 oz) dried semolina

1 sage leaf

Salt and pepper

SERVES 4–8

APRONS ON, LET'S COOK!

1 Parboil the potatoes by placing them in a saucepan of cold water, bringing to the boil, and simmering for 6–8 minutes.

2 Melt the butter and oil in a large non-stick pan over a medium heat. Sauté the onions and (drained) potato chunks for 1–2 minutes. Don't worry if the potatoes break down.

3 Pour in the stock, sweetcorn, cream and semolina and stir well. Add the sage leaf and stir again. Ask your child to stir too (under careful supervision).

4 Gently simmer for about 20 minutes. Then blitz until smooth in a blender or food processor (you may need to do this in batches so as not to overload). Season to taste before serving.

GOURMET FOR GROWN-UPS

Two words – cayenne pepper. When adding the stock, also add about ¼ tsp of cayenne for a good kick; ½ tsp if you like things seriously hot! This is perfect when served warm in mugs, blankets over shoulders, on Guy Fawkes Night or at Halloween.

SWEET SPICED SUNSHINE CAKES

Sounds strange? I once cooked these up for a Farmers Market, offered samples (along with a selection of brownies and cupcakes) and the corn cakes definitely held their own. The polenta adds a nice bit of texture and adds to the sunshine hue.

COOKERY SKILLS: I CAN PRACTISE SIFTING FLOUR AND WHISKING EGGS

SHOPPING LIST

85 g (3 oz) butter or margarine

150 g (5 oz) sweetcorn

200 g (7 oz) plain flour

1 tsp baking powder

100 g (3½ oz) golden caster sugar

100 g (3½ oz) dried polenta

2 eggs

100 ml (3½ fl oz) milk

300 ml (½ pint) soured cream

1 tsp brown sugar

¼ tsp cinnamon

MAKES 20

APRONS ON, LET'S COOK!

1 Preheat the oven to 180°C/ 350° F/gas 4 and line two muffin trays with 20 paper muffin cases.

2 Melt the butter or margarine in a small frying pan over a medium heat and add the sweetcorn, letting them sweat for 1–2 minutes. Set aside.

3 Your child/ren could help with this step. Sift the flour and baking powder into a large bowl and stir in the sugar and polenta.

4 Whisk the eggs. Add them to the dry ingredients along with the milk, soured cream, sweetcorn and melted butter or margarine. Stir gently to combine.

5 Spoon the mixture carefully and equally into the paper cases. Bake for 20–22 minutes in the preheated oven until golden and a skewer or toothpick comes out clean. Leave to rest still in the hot trays for another 10 minutes, on top of the hob (out of reach of kids).

6 Take each corn cake out of the tin and leave to cool completely on a wire rack. Ask a child to combine the brown sugar and cinnamon in a small dish, then, using their fingers, dust a small amount over the cooled cakes before serving. This step could also be done while the cakes are actually cooling.

GOURMET FOR GROWN-UPS

Skip the spicy topping, replace the sugar for approx 75 g (3 oz) grated hard cheese, stir-fry the sweetcorn with some chopped onion and chopped red chillies and serve warm with Mexican chilli as a 'bread' side dish.

peppers

MARKETING PEPPERS

My absolute favourite way of marketing peppers is to play on their shape and inner hollows by creating pepperpots to drink from. Simply cut off the top of a pepper, hollow out the inside, and fill with juice. Then hand the pepper-pot to your child and invite them to drink from it. The fact that their mouths will be touching the 'cups' is in itself a big step for some kids. You can then invite them to be really silly and, using their teeth, nibble a little pattern around the tops of their cups.

TRY THIS...

Feed small chunks of different coloured peppers onto a piece of string that you can then use as a 'bracelet' to tie round your child's wrist, encouraging them to nibble on each colour (like those sweetie necklaces I used to love as a kid). I've also found peppers work really well (when finely chopped) in sandwiches. They're good buddies with any of the following: cream cheese, hummus, grated hard cheese or egg mayo. I'm sure you can think of more...

HUMMUS IN A HURRY

This is quick, quick, quick – and I make no apologies for the blatant short-cut (though if you do want to roast your own red peppers, be my guest). This is quite a dry mix – feel free to loosen with a bit of extra olive oil if you think you'll have more success that way. By the way it's another fantastic food buddy for the Tortilla Chips (see page 93). In emergencies, I have made this without the tahini – although it tastes less 'hummusy' and is a little drier. You'll need a blender or food processor for this recipe.

COOKERY SKILLS: I CAN USE A KNIFE TO SPREAD HUMMUS ONTO TOAST

SHOPPING LIST

75 g (3 oz) tinned chickpeas, drained

50 g (2 oz) roasted red peppers from a jar

1–2 tbsp good-quality olive oil

1 tbsp tahini

2 tsp fresh lemon juice

A pinch of salt

SERVES 4–8

APRONS ON, LET'S COOK!

1 Put everything in a blender or food processor and really blitz until very smooth. So your child feels involved, maybe they could help 'chop' the peppers up a bit with a plastic knife or stir all the ingredients together before blending.

GOURMET FOR GROWN-UPS

Add a little chilli powder, cayenne pepper or paprika for a bit of a kick. Caramelized red onions also make a great hummus topping.

RED PEPPER PIZZAS

This isn't the quickest recipe in the world – but you can cook up a big batch and freeze the sauce. I don't like removing the pepper skins as I know that any bright colours in vegetables carry high levels of vitamins and antioxidants – so I created this recipe in order to keep the skins firmly on. While you could skip the olives, try and keep them in as they are full of those healthy omega oils we keep reading about (but use olives in oil rather than salty brine). The sauce also works as a good basic 'red' pasta sauce, just stir through with your child's favourite pasta and top off with cheese. As your child becomes more accustomed to liking the flavour, you can create a chunkier sauce – until eventually you may barely need to blend it.

COOKERY SKILLS: I CAN LEARN HOW TO SLICE VEGETABLES AND USE A ROLLING PIN

SHOPPING LIST

4 red peppers

A glug of olive oil

1 garlic clove, finely chopped

1 onion, finely chopped

1 x 400 g (13 oz) tin chopped tomatoes

100 g (3½ oz) sun-blush tomatoes

2 tsp brown sugar

A pinch of salt

50 g (2 oz) pitted green or black olives (optional)

A generous handful of fresh basil

1 x pack of ready-to-roll puff pastry (at room temperature)

About 150 g (5 oz) goats' cheese (or mozzarella or ricotta)

SERVES 8

APRONS ON, LET'S COOK!

1 Cut the red peppers into long thin strips. If they're old enough, allow your child to help. Give them the base of the pepper that you don't really need – you don't necessarily need to use their efforts in the recipe if they're not sliced finely enough. Remember to casually pick up a few bits of pepper as you go and eagerly eat them.

2 Put a good glug of olive oil in a large, non-stick lidded saucepan over a medium–high heat. Once it starts to heat, add the garlic and onions and sauté for a couple of minutes.

3 Add the strips of red pepper. Stir through, turn down the heat to low–medium and cover with the lid. You want the pepper strips to cook through and soften. This will take about 20 minutes – but do stir (with a wooden spoon) from time to time.

4 Once the peppers are nice and soft, add the chopped tomatoes, sun-blush tomatoes, sugar, salt and olives. Keep the lid off, turn up the heat if necessary and allow to simmer for about 6–8 minutes until the sauce thickens. Keep stirring so nothing sticks. Obviously keep children away from the hob at this stage for safety.

5 Once the sauce has thickened remove from the heat and allow to cool slightly. Then add in the basil and stir through.

6 Finally, whizz it up in the blender or food processor as smooth as you can. Taste it and adjust the seasoning if necessary. The sauce is now ready to use as a pasta sauce or pizza base. Once cool it can be frozen at this stage.

7 Preheat your oven to 220°C/425°F/gas 7. Roll out the puff pastry on a lightly floured surface to a thickness of 5 mm and cut out four equal squares.

8 Take each square and roll so they're thinner still (about 2–3 mm) and cut out even squares of approx 8–10 cm (3½ –4 in) on all sides.

9 Gently trace a smaller square within each little square (about 1–2 cm/½–1 in inside the square) – so the knife doesn't cut, just leaves a mark – and with a fork, prick the inner square a few times. Glaze the outer edge with a bit of milk (or beaten egg) if you want.

10 Fill the inner square with a teaspoon of the red pepper sauce and then a few chunks of the goats' cheese (or a plainer cheese).

11 Place in the preheated oven and cook for 8–10 minutes until the puff pastry is cooked through and the cheese is browned and bubbly.

PUFF PASTRY TIPS

• Puff pastry needs good strong heat to 'puff out' – so preheat your oven for at least 20 minutes.
• Always use a sharp knife to cut it and cut in straight lines, not angles (otherwise you risk rupturing the in-built 'layers' that characterise puff pastry).
• For this same reason, don't roll together and re-use any scraps left-over.

GOURMET FOR GROWN-UPS

These would be very stylish canapés for a party. Experiment with different cheeses, garnish with sprigs of fresh basil, and add tiny morsels of smoked bacon to the sauce.

pumpkin and squash

MARKETING PUMPKIN AND SQUASH

I often wonder why people don't cook with squash or pumpkin more often. For starters both have lots of natural sweetness so appeal to a child's natural sweet tooth. You can also mash them (when cooked) very easily into potato – it blends particularly well with sweet potato (quite literally due to their shared orange hue) and is a perfect partner with any chicken dish (chicken and squash risotto is just gorgeous – especially with a creamy blue cheese stirred through too). I think though I've figured out why people avoid it: *they hate preparing it!* I mean, really, who has the time to do all that peeling and chopping? (See my tip, below.)

I can think of no better way to market a pumpkin than to indulge in a little pumpkin carving arts-and-crafts style. I'd also recommend carving out a small round-shaped squash or pumpkin and using it as an actual bowl for a delicious, warming soup – if it's a squash/pumpkin soup, all the better (or try roasted squash and sweet potato).

66 *Fiona is the Harry Potter of vegetables; she can do magical things with them!* 99

Laura Goldman, mum to Sam (aged 6)

TRY THIS...

My best tip for squash and pumpkin is not to peel them first – but to bung them into a hot oven and roast them, skins on, until a sharp knife goes through easily. Then allow them to cool before cutting up easily – and a lot more safely I think than trying to cut and peel a vegetable that, when raw, is hard and unyielding.

SQUASHY SCONES

This is a fantastic recipe for kids – but very messy! I usually serve these warm, almost straight from the oven – they're a great kid's lunchbox idea too. Add the tiniest pinch of nutmeg if you fancy (about ¼ teaspoon) – or even some chopped walnuts (for older kids; and check for nut allergies obviously). You will also need cookie cutters for this recipe.

COOKERY SKILLS: I CAN LEARN HOW TO RUB BUTTER INTO FLOUR AND PRACTISE CUTTING OUT SHAPES WITH A CUTTER

SHOPPING LIST

215 g (7½ oz) plain flour, plus extra for dusting

50 g (2 oz) golden caster sugar

1 tbsp baking powder

50 g (2 oz) unsalted butter (not too hard, not too soft)

300 g (10 oz) cooked butternut squash flesh (peeled, no seeds), mashed right down

60 ml (2½ fl oz) milk, at room temperature

**MAKES ABOUT
10 SCONES**

APRONS ON, LET'S COOK!

1 Preheat the oven to 200°C/400°F/gas 6.

2 Sift the flour, sugar and baking powder into a large bowl – get a child to help.

3 Rub the butter into the flour mix using your fingertips – again, a child will enjoy this. The mix will soon start to resemble breadcrumbs.

4 Now add the squash and milk and with a large metal spoon (or hands!), stir until it's all combined.

5 Flour a large chopping board and turn out the mix. Flour your hands – and any child's (clean) hands – and simply press the mix out until it's about 1 cm (½ in) in depth all over.

6 Using a shape cutter (of about 7 cm (3 in) in diameter) cut out your scones (kids will love doing this) and ask a child to place each onto a lightly greased tray.

7 Place in the preheated oven for about 10–12 minutes or until they're slightly golden and raised. Leave to cool on a wire rack.

GOURMET FOR GROWN-UPS

The scones are a tea-time treat for all ages really. But you could add some bling by serving as an alternative cream tea, Devon style. Use low-fat crème fraîche and in-season berries that have been slightly squished and sweetened with a small dash of vanilla sugar.

BUTTERNUT AND BANANA SMOOTHIE

Strangely this is one of my proudest recipes (which may surprise some as it's so simple it's more an idea than a recipe). When you think about their natural sweetness, squash – and pumpkin – are perfect veggie-partners for fruit smoothies. If your kids absolutely will not eat veg, but love fruit smoothies, then this is the recipe for you. You'll need a blender or food processor for this recipe.

COOKERY SKILLS: I CAN PRACTISE MASHING AND CHOPPING

SHOPPING LIST

25 g (1 oz) cooked squash or pumpkin, peeled and cooled (see my tip on page 48)

1 large banana, peeled. Ask a child to chop it up

150 g (5 oz) pineapple, skin off (or tinned as long as it's in juice and not syrup)

300 ml (½ pint) fresh orange juice

3 dessertspoons low-fat live yogurt or crème fraîche

MAKES ENOUGH FOR 4 KIDS

APRONS ON, LET'S COOK!

1 Ask your child to help mash the cooked squash or pumpkin up a bit and also to chop the banana – kid's plastic blunt knives are perfect for this.

2 Then put all of the ingredients in the blender or food processor, blitz until smooth and serve.

GOURMET FOR GROWN-UPS

Am I really going to suggest (in a kids' cookbook) that you could add a dash of rum to the smoothie, replace the orange juice with pineapple juice and then a splash of coconut milk? (Yes, sort of!) Piña Colada with Butternut Squash! Now there's a recipe idea I bet you never thought you'd see in print – please don't mix up the kid's batch with the adult's though!

potatoes

MARKETING POTATOES

It's worth reminding any crisp-addict kids that (most) crisps are actually made from potatoes – and while you're at it, try my quick recipe below for homemade crisps. Potatoes are ideal for some good old-fashioned paint printers. Cut a potato in half, blot the cut-side dry with some kitchen roll, draw a simple shape, cut out the background and hey presto! Get your kids to dip the shapes in paint and create fun pictures or greeting cards etc. Potatoes are very easy to grow too – and kids usually love finding that 'buried treasure' beneath the soil when helping in the garden.

TRY THIS...

Try these homemade crips! Slice a peeled potato until the slices are wafer-thin (a mandolin makes this pretty do-able). Wash the slices with cold water to remove any starch and gently dry them with a tea towel. Heat a pan with hot vegetable oil (follow the frying guidelines on page 86 for my aubergine crispies) and add the potato slices, frying them until lightly browned. Drain on kitchen roll to get rid of any excess oil. Sprinkle lightly with a little salt before serving.

POTATO PILLOWS

One young mum once approached me and was in despair that the only 'potato' product her son would eat was chips. These were inspired by that conversation; creating something that looked like a chip – and had a bit of crunch and texture – but that pulled together the essence of a potato. Sounds a bit airy-fairy? Try these and you'll see what I mean.

COOKERY SKILLS: I CAN PRACTISE MASHING POTATOES AND USING A ROLLING PIN

SHOPPING LIST

500 g (1 lb) peeled and chopped potatoes

30 g (2 oz) butter

2 egg yolks

½ tsp salt (use ¼ tsp for 1–3-year-olds)

110 g (3½ oz) self-raising flour, plus extra for dusting

SERVES 4–6

APRONS ON, LET'S COOK!

1 Cover the potatoes with water, add a pinch of salt, bring to the boil and simmer until cooked through. This should take about 15 minutes.

2 Drain the potatoes and return them to the pan. Ask a child to add the butter, egg yolks and salt – both of you mash it all together thoroughly.

3 Transfer to a big bowl, ask a child to add the flour and, with a big metal spoon, mix until it becomes a stodgy dough-type mix. Leave in the fridge to thoroughly cool down and firm up for a good 2 hours or so.

4 Preheat the oven to 200°C/400°F/gas 6 and oil a baking tray.

5 Thoroughly flour a surface – and your hands and a rolling pin – and roll the mix out to about 1 cm (½ in) thickness. Carefully cut out chip-sized quantities – I usually make mine about 8 cm (3½ in) long, 2 cm (1 in) wide.

6 Place the chips on the prepared tray and ask a child to brush them with a little olive oil (perhaps sprinkle with a little bit of finely grated Parmesan cheese too). Bake for around 10–15 minutes until golden and crispy – I prefer them slightly over-cooked to under.

GOURMET FOR GROWN-UPS

Add grated Parmesan to the mash and sprinkle with sea salt and chillies before baking. Bake until really crisp and serve with homemade ketchup, sweet chilli sauce or an aioli dip. The 'chips' could be wrapped in baskets of parchment paper, covered with newspaper – chip shop style!

SWEET POTATO AND PECAN PANCAKES

These are a lovely weekend brunch idea – and one that a few of my Toddler Chef dads have enjoyed doing with their kids at the weekend. After all, the kitchen is a great place to chat, listen to music and just have a little 'bonding' time. This is a nice little intro to nuts as well.

COOKERY SKILLS: I CAN LEARN HOW TO FLIP PANCAKES

SHOPPING LIST

325 g (11 oz) cooked sweet potato, mashed (about 3–4 sweet potatoes)

200 g (7 oz) plain flour

1 tsp baking powder

½ tsp cinnamon

50 g (2 oz) golden caster sugar

50 g (2 oz) pecans or walnuts, chopped (optional)

2 eggs, whisked

15 g (½ oz) butter, melted, plus extra for frying

250 ml (8 fl oz) milk

MAKES APPROXIMATELY 24 SMALL PANCAKES

APRONS ON, LET'S COOK!

1 Set aside the cooked and mashed potato to cool. You could cook up a big batch then freeze the additional mash for another time.

2 Get your kids to help with the following: sift together the flour, baking powder and cinnamon into a big mixing bowl. Stir through the sugar and chopped nuts.

3 Add the eggs, butter and half the milk and stir through to combine. Add the remainder of the milk and stir through.

4 Finally mix in the sweet potato mash.

5 Melt a small knob of butter in a non-stick pan over a medium–high heat. Add a dollop of the mix to the pan (I usually keep these quite small – perhaps 8 cm (3½ in) diameter). Cook for 2–3 minutes, turning with a spatula – or flipping! – until golden and cooked through.

NOTE
Always check for any nut allergies. Young babies should not be offered nuts.

GOURMET FOR GROWN-UPS

Add more spice to give these an adult kick, another ½ tsp nutmeg and (perhaps) the same again of ginger. Serve with bacon or sausages and some maple syrup for an American-style breakfast.

avocado

MARKETING AVOCADO

If I had to choose just one of these 25 foods for you to convert your kids to, this would be it (with broccoli coming in a very close second). Avocados are one of the most amazing superfoods – full of healthy omega oils, which are good for concentration and brain development amongst other things. Trouble is, kids don't really care about omegas and essential oils – and I'm the first to admit that avocados are an acquired taste (though I happen to really like them). Two tips: never buy them over-ripe (brown, bruised and squishy – eugh); and never buy them under-ripe (hard, bland and almost impossible to cut from their skins). Play up to the pretty soft green that lies inside the tough brown exterior.

TRY THIS...

One of the easiest ways to get your kids into avocados is to mash half an avocado with a (ripe) banana – ta-da instant sandwich filler! (Best eaten straightaway before it turns brown). Or try chopping (or blending) avocado with various soft, sweet fruits (such as strawberries and peaches), add a squeeze of lime and you have instant fruity guacamole (or a great yogurt topping)!

❝ *Avocado ice cream? Are you kidding me?! Once again, Fiona's recipes ring true. Everyone in the class loved it.* **❞**

Sarah Kelly

ELSIE'S AVOCADO ICE CREAM

This can also be blended with one or two mashed bananas but I actually prefer it without. You will need a blender or food processor for this recipe and ideally an electric whisk as well. My youngest daughter (who does have a very sweet tooth) loves this.

COOKERY SKILLS: I CAN HELP CHOOSE PERFECTLY RIPE AVOCADOS

SHOPPING LIST

4 (ripe) avocados – ask a child to help you take these out of their skins and chop them up a bit.

Juice of 2 limes

300 ml (½ pint) double cream

200 g (7 oz) caster sugar

½ tsp vanilla extract

SERVES 10–15

APRONS ON, LET'S COOK!

1 Place the avocado and lime juice in a blender or food processor and whizz up until thoroughly smooth.

2 Put the avocado-lime mix in a food processor with a whisk attachment, add the double cream, caster sugar and vanilla extract and whisk on a medium–high setting for about 3 minutes. You could do this with a hand-held electric whisk or by hand but it'll take longer.

3 Place in a container (perhaps recycle an ice-cream tub?) and transfer to the freezer for 3–4 hours. Any longer and it's a bit hard to scoop out – this isn't in itself a detriment to the recipe – just remember to let it thaw slightly before serving for a creamier 'soft scoop' effect.

NOTE
If an avocado is slightly unripe, place it in a paper bag overnight with some ripe fruit, such as apples or bananas.

GOURMET FOR GROWN-UPS

I served this once at a garden party in posh ice-cream cones, covered in chopped pistachios and a sprinkling of lime zest. They did draw gasps for prettiness alone.

SUSHI SANDWICHES

My contribution to Italian–Japanese fusion cooking – and I use that term very tongue-in-cheek! These are a bit fiddly to make, but are a nice, easy intro to avocado. Plus kids will enjoy rolling out the bread and helping you layer the fillings. Feel free to use a different cheese – and tomato ketchup would work in place of the fresh tomato – though I'm not the biggest fan of ketchup so tend not to use it much in recipes. If your child enjoys these, I'd progress to a proper tricolour toasted sandwich.

COOKERY SKILLS: I CAN PRACTISE MY ROLLING PIN SKILLS

SHOPPING LIST

2 slices of bread,
crusts cut off

½ ripe avocado

1–2 tsp green pesto

Thinly sliced mozzarella
cheese (enough to cover
two slices of bread)

1 ripe, juicy tomato,
chopped

SERVES 2–3

AS A SNACK

APRONS ON, LET'S COOK!

1 Using a rolling pin, flatten out each slice of bread in turn. Kids will love this job – and any/all of the following ones.

2 Mash up the avocado until it's very smooth and then mix in the pesto sauce.

3 Spread the avocado-pesto mix on both slices of bread, follow with the mozzarella – just dot it about – then the tomato.

4 Carefully roll up each slice into a sausage shape. Take a small bit of cling film and wrap up the 'sausages', fairly tightly but carefully, twisting both ends of cling film to secure.

5 Chill in the freezer for about 15 minutes (this way the sandwiches become firmer and easier to cut).

6 Unwrap the 'sausages' and slice little pinwheels, about 2.5 cm (1 in) long. Serve on their sides so your kids can see the three colours.

GOURMET FOR GROWN-UPS

Using the toastie idea I mention above, add parma ham, fresh basil, and sun-dried tomatoes – a delicious, Italian inspired lunch!

spinach

MARKETING SPINACH

Just as broccoli has become broccoli 'trees', spinach has a Faulkner alter-ego as 'magical leaves'. It's not unknown in Toddler Chef workshops for me to hold these 'leaves' as a Tree of Knowledge, swaying in the wind, asking kids various questions and inviting them to pick a 'leaf' to gobble up as a prize. One worth trying at home perhaps?!

TRY THIS...

Wilt some spinach in a pan (or cook up some frozen spinach), blend it up in a blender or food processor, allow to cool, then fold into mayonnaise. This is a really good little sandwich filler when used with grated cheese or mashed up boiled egg. Play up to the funky green colour.

Alternatively, try creating a spinach 'bento box' (Japanese style) by wrapping other foods into spinach leaves, tying – as parcels – with a string of celery and placing side by side. You could use the same technique for lettuce (leaf) 'wrappers'. Also try shredding little bits of spinach in with mint and buttery new potatoes.

> ❝ Matilda's absolute favourite game has been The Tree of Knowledge. An ingenious way to get kids eating spinach. ❞
>
> **Jackie Sparks, mum to Matilda (aged 2)**

SPINACH PESTO

This is another personal favourite and a real crowd-pleaser – especially with other mums post play-dates where you can announce that you got all the kids eating fresh spinach for tea! Do get any kids helping hands-on with weighing and measuring. You will need a blender or food processor for this recipe.

COOKERY SKILLS: I CAN PRACTISE SQUEEZING FRUIT FOR JUICE.

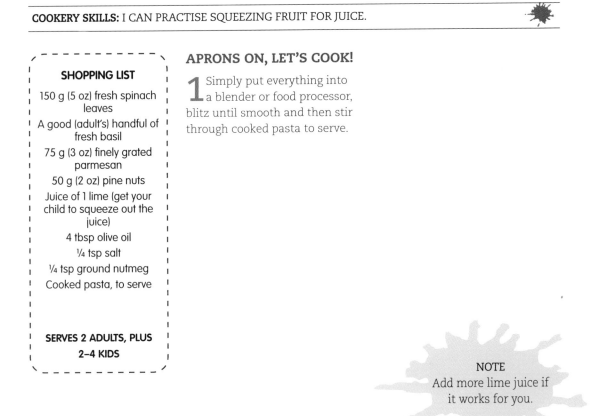

SHOPPING LIST

150 g (5 oz) fresh spinach leaves

A good (adult's) handful of fresh basil

75 g (3 oz) finely grated parmesan

50 g (2 oz) pine nuts

Juice of 1 lime (get your child to squeeze out the juice)

4 tbsp olive oil

¼ tsp salt

¼ tsp ground nutmeg

Cooked pasta, to serve

SERVES 2 ADULTS, PLUS 2–4 KIDS

APRONS ON, LET'S COOK!

1 Simply put everything into a blender or food processor, blitz until smooth and then stir through cooked pasta to serve.

NOTE
Add more lime juice if it works for you.

GOURMET FOR GROWN-UPS

Replace the pine nuts with pistachios. It won't drastically affect the flavour – but you can impress guests by announcing you're serving pasta with 'homemade spinach, lime and pistachio pesto' – now who wouldn't want to casually name-drop that one?

SPINACH, FETA AND CRANBERRY PARCELS

I love these, and generally have a variation of them every year at Christmas time. This may seem quite a 'sophisticated' recipe for a youngster but in fact it's very simple – both in concept and preparation. What really counts is the reaction and most kids in my workshops do enjoy these (I think the cranberries help in carrying the marketing and it's very easy to create a fairy story – or PR campaign – around the idea of looking inside a parcel: 'ooh, look, little rubies… and forest leaves from the fairies… and sparkly snow!' I'm sure you get the idea).

COOKERY SKILLS: I CAN PRACTISE MASHING AND CHOPPING.

SHOPPING LIST

1 tbsp olive oil

1 small onion, very finely chopped

1 bag of fresh spinach, about 200 g (7 oz), or your own home-grown

200 g (7 oz) feta cheese, crumbled or in small chunks

50 g (2 oz) dried cranberries

10 sheets ready-made filo pastry

50 g (2 oz) butter, melted (or some olive oil)

Salt and pepper

MAKES ABOUT 10

APRONS ON, LET'S COOK!

1 Heat the oil in a large pan over medium–high and sauté the onion for a couple of minutes.

2 Add half the spinach, allow it to wilt down – help it with a wooden spoon. Add the rest of the spinach and do the same again. Keep the heat pretty low. After a few minutes the spinach will reduce right back in size. Careful kids can help with all this.

3 Take the pan off the heat and stir through all the cheese. Then add the cranberries. Season with a little salt and set aside.

4 Preheat the oven to 200°C/ 400° F/gas 6.

5 Carefully take one sheet of filo pastry (I find that a sheet sized about 25 cm x 25 cm/ 10 in x 10 in is a good size). Ask a child to brush the sheet all over with some melted butter and then turn the buttery side over, placing it directly on the baking tray itself, buttery side down.

6 Place a dessertspoon-sized quantity of the spinach mix in the middle and then literally fold up the pastry like a parcel – top bit over, bottom bit over, one side, the other side. Again, this is a brilliant job for kids (remember to play up to it being a magical parcel).

7 Keep going like this, spacing the parcels out once they've all been folded up. You may need two baking trays. Bake for about 10 minutes until golden brown.

GOURMET FOR GROWN-UPS

This is the one recipe I struggled to 'gourmet' because I happen to think they're very nice as they are. I suppose you could vary the presentation of the filo (hmm, too fiddly?). I have had success in the past by ditching the cranberries and adding a dollop of a delicious homemade chutney.

leeks and greens

MARKETING LEEKS AND GREENS

One of my most successful Toddler Chef games has been the Five Senses Game – and to be honest, you can utilise pretty much any food within this game, including crunchy carrot (to hear), jelly (to touch), chocolate (to taste), papaya (to see inside) and basil (to smell). Here I'm adapting the game for green vegetables. Feel free to tweak my suggestions.

THE FIVE SENSES GAME

• Lay out the following (washed and cut up where necessary) in little bowls but don't allow your child to see: cucumber, celery, broad beans, runner beans, mange tout.
• Ask your child to identify each vegetable based on their five senses (blindfold them when necessary).

1 Smell the cucumber
2 Listen to the crunchy celery
3 Look at the broad beans as we open them to reveal what's inside
4 Feel the furry runner beans and their pods
5 Taste the mange tout

TRY THIS...

One 'green' that most Brits are hard-wired to hate are Brussell sprouts. Personally, I love them. Try sprouts – or any other green veg – sliced up, raw, in a 'green coleslaw' with grated carrot, sliced spring onion and a little low-fat mayo.

When it comes to leeks, good old-fashioned leek and potato soup is usually a winner in our house (and you can find countless recipes either online or in various cookery books) – or cheat and buy a good-quality fresh soup in a carton.

GREEN BEAN POLENTA CHIPS

This is one of my favourite recipes – if only because it uses a much under-rated grain, polenta. In this respect we're almost road-testing two foods here – polenta and green beans. You could deep-fry these (for speed) – but personally I'd need a more compelling reason to load these up with excess fat. They're beautifully crispy from the oven, I promise.

COOKERY SKILLS: I CAN PRACTISE CHOPPING VEGETABLES.

SHOPPING LIST

500 ml (17 fl oz) light vegetable stock – use only half of the powder/cube that the pack tells you to
65 g (2½ oz) fine green beans
125 g (4 oz) polenta grains
35 g (1½ oz) grated Italian cheese, such as Parmesan
Olive oil, for greasing

SERVES 4–6

GOURMET FOR GROWN-UPS

Cut the polenta into triangles and use as a base that you can add toppings to – such as caramelised onion and crumbled blue cheese or garlic porcini mushrooms – pizza-style!

APRONS ON, LET'S COOK!

1 Grease a baking tray and set aside.

2 Put the prepared stock in a saucepan and bring to a fast simmer, stirring with a wooden spoon to dissolve any granules.

3 Meanwhile put the green beans in a pan of water, bring to the boil and then simmer for 2–3 minutes until tender. Drain. Chop up into small pieces Set aside.

4 Take the stock off the heat for a moment and turn the heat right down. The following is really a job for an adult, though obviously your child can watch. In a slow, steady stream, add the polenta, stirring quickly as it hits the water.

5 Once it's all in, put the pan back on the low heat and keep stirring for about 10 minutes. It will become a dry 'mush' (no other word for it!) and is good exercise for those arm muscles!

6 Take the polenta off the heat and stir through the cheese and then the finely chopped green beans. Quickly turn it all out onto the prepared tray. Use a spoon (or other implement to pat it down). Within a few quick moments this will be cool enough so you can use your hands to tease it into a rectangular shape – about 1 cm (½ in) in depth – I usually get mine to about 20 cm x 15 cm (8 in x 6 in) in length/width.

7 Once it's properly cool transfer to the fridge to fully cool and set for an hour or so.

8 Preheat the oven to 200°C/400°F/gas 6. Generously grease another baking tray with olive oil. Turn the polenta out onto a chopping board, then slice into reasonably thick 'fries' – about 2 cm x 7 cm (1 in x 3 in).

9 Place on the second baking tray then cook in the oven for about 15 minutes. Using a spatula, turn the fries over and cook for another 5 minutes until golden. Serve with a dip as a snack or as a side-dish as you would serve chips.

NOTE
You could also grill these, on both sides until golden.

65

CRISPY LEEK AND CHEDDAR MUFFINS

Granted, not every parent is desperate for their kid to fall in love with leeks – but this recipe works on a couple of levels: firstly, it introduces your kids to the taste of onion (leeks are from the same family) and therefore 'stronger' flavours. Secondly, it continues to market 'green' foods by putting this particular green food in a child-friendly recipe idea, such as muffins. These taste best when sliced in half, still slightly warm, spread with butter. I tend to use these a lot in my kids' lunchboxes.

COOKERY SKILLS: I CAN PRACTISE SIFTING FLOUR AND BREAKING AND WHISKING EGGS

SHOPPING LIST

1 leek

15 g (½ oz) butter

225 g (7½ oz) self-raising flour

1 tsp mustard powder

100 g (3½ oz) medium Cheddar cheese, grated

1 egg

150 ml (¼ pint) milk

50 ml (2 fl oz) olive oil

Pinch of salt

MAKES 10

APRONS ON, LET'S COOK!

1 Preheat the oven to 180°C/ 350° F/gas 4. Thoroughly grease a muffin baking tin.

2 Finely slice the leek until you have about 100 g (3½ oz) of slices.

3 Melt the butter in a pan and sauté the leeks for about 2–3 minutes over a medium–high heat. They will break up and reduce as you stir them round but don't worry about that.

4 Ask a child to sift together the flour, salt and mustard powder into a bowl. Also get them to stir through the cheese and beat the egg in a separate bowl.

5 Whizz up the buttery leek mix in a blender or food processor so that the leeks break up some more. Once your kids are used to eating leeks you can leave them as chunkier pieces.

6 Add the milk and oil to the beaten egg, then pour into the dry ingredients. Add the blitzed leeks and stir through.

7 Divide the mixture equally into 10 of the muffin tray holes (you can use muffin paper cases if you want) and cook for about 18 minutes in the preheated oven. Once out of the oven, leave in the tray for a further 10 minutes. Turn each muffin out to cool slightly on a wire rack.

GOURMET FOR GROWN-UPS

Serve as above but with flavoured butter, such as garlic and parsley.

cauliflower and courgettes

MARKETING CAULIFLOWER AND COURGETTES

Just as broccoli stems are green trees, cauliflower can just as easily be marketed as snowy white trees. This is an experimental technique, but sometimes allowing kids to create 'finger patterns' with sauces and blended foods (such as the cauliflower cheese mash here) can be effective. Basically they create patterns on the plate with their fingers and you can then encourage them to 'lick your fingers clean!' If you're lucky enough to get hold of a freshly picked courgette with its flower still intact, this is as good a 'marketing tool' as any other I can think of (try using a stuffed courgette flower recipe). Meanwhile, if your child is a fan of cucumber, try serving (raw) courgette slices in the same way as you would cucumber – perhaps with cucumber. Compare the two in taste and texture.

TRY THIS...

Get your child to help you pull off little cauliflower florets that you can then use as croutons in soup – or lightly stir-fry them then add to pasta dishes (or even use on top of

" Finally I got Edward eating courgette today! "

Sally Pattison, mum to Edward (aged 5)

pizza). Courgettes can be made pretty (as cucumbers often are) by running a fork down the skin, all the way around, then slicing them up. Serve the slices raw in salads with a blue cheese dressing. Or try grilling finely sliced courgette and adding these as pizza toppings.

CAULIFLOWER CHEESE MASH

I love this recipe. So simple but a real favourite with lots of the kids I work with. Cauliflower goes really smooth in a blender and this is a great alternative to mashed potato. As your child (hopefully) progresses with this recipe you can start making it chunkier and chunkier until – effectively – you have a more conventional cauliflower cheese dish. You will need a blender or food processor for this recipe.

COOKERY SKILLS: I CAN PREPARE CAULIFLOWER

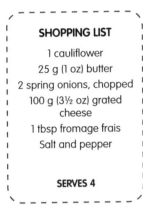

SHOPPING LIST

1 cauliflower

25 g (1 oz) butter

2 spring onions, chopped

100 g (3½ oz) grated cheese

1 tbsp fromage frais

Salt and pepper

SERVES 4

APRONS ON, LET'S COOK!

1 Entice your child to pull the green leaves off the cauliflower. Let them play around a bit with the leaves ('can you stick them on your nose or use them as fans etc?')

2 Again, with your child's help, pull off florets into a saucepan. Cover with cold water, bring to a boil, then simmer until the cauliflower is tender – this should take about 15 minutes.

3 Once the cauliflower has been cooking for 10–15 minutes, melt the butter in a pan, add the spring onion and sauté for 1–2 minutes.

4 Drain the cauliflower, return to the pan and mash (a child might like to help). Add the butter and sautéed onion and stir through.

5 Place it all in a blender or food processor and whizz up until smooth. Transfer back to the pan and – over a low heat – stir through the cheese, fromage frais and seasoning (not too much salt).

NOTE
Try serving this with breaded fish or your child's favourite sausages.

GOURMET FOR GROWN-UPS

Use blue cheese in this recipe for a slightly more mature taste, and perhaps stir through some chopped walnuts.

COURGETTE AND LIME SORBET

I was inspired to make this following a glut of courgettes that had grown in our garden. Don't be tempted to skip the mint leaves –they create a lovely bit of flavour here. You will need a blender or food processor for this recipe.

COOKERY SKILLS: I CAN PRACTISE SCOOPING OUT SEEDS

SHOPPING LIST

1 courgette

2 limes

75 g (3 oz) caster sugar

2 fresh mint leaves

MAKES ENOUGH FOR 4 EAGER KIDS

APRONS ON, LET'S COOK!

1 Slice the courgette in half lengthways and, using a teaspoon, scoop out any visible seeds. The kids could help with the scooping part.

2 Chop the courgette into small-ish pieces – again, the kids could help here with a safe knife. They could also help to squeeze the juice of both limes.

3 Put the courgettes, lime juice, sugar, and mint leaves in a blender or food processor and blitz until smooth.

4 Transfer the mixture to individual dishes and place in the freezer for about 1½ hours.

GOURMET FOR GROWN-UPS

Serve with fresh sprigs of mint in sugar-rimmed cocktail glasses.
Simple but elegant.

slightly sour fruit

MARKETING SOUR FRUIT

By 'sour' fruit I mean fruit that is less conventionally sweet – rhubarb, apple, citrus and kiwi fruits, for example. These are often less obviously marketed towards kids. How about creating a 'funny fruit' chart with your kids to figure out what's in season and where you might find some of these less popular fruits. You can have fun together by seeking them out and sampling the different tastes.

TRY THIS...

Is it me, or are apples these days being shunned by parents in favour of bananas, strawberries and grapes? Don't get me wrong, I love all of the above (in fact I can't think of a fruit that I dislike at all) but apples – for kids – have gone off the boil a bit lately. Try this as a little quick-kids-cuisine: core an apple (a proper apple corer is the best way to do this) and fill with a mix of ricotta cheese, mashed banana and other chopped fruits. Bake in the oven and serve warm with vanilla ice cream.

CREAMY RHUBARB MOCKTAIL

This is pure indulgence in a glass! Serve chilled. You will need a blender or food processor for this recipe.

COOKERY SKILLS: I CAN PRACTISE SQUEEZING THE JUICE FROM FRUIT

APRONS ON, LET'S COOK!

1 Slice the orange in half and squeeze its juice by hand – or rather, ask your child to. Get them to really get their (clean) fingers up and into that flesh.

2 Place the rhubarb, apple, orange juice and sugar into a large saucepan. Turn the heat up pretty high. When you hear it start to bubble a bit – ask your child to listen too – bring the heat down and simmer for about 6–7 minutes until the rhubarb is tender. Give a stir now and again.

3 Allow the mixture to cool slightly, then put it in the blender or food processor with the milk and cream. Whizz up then set aside to cool completely. Decant into a jug and transfer to the fridge until needed.

NOTE
Why not re-create these as ice lollies too? Simply pour the mix into ice lolly moulds and freeze overnight!

GOURMET FOR GROWN-UPS

Just add alcohol! Vodka works especially well.

KIWI AND LIME CUPCAKES

We're tackling two sour fruits here: kiwi and lime (although I know that ripe kiwi can also taste very sweet). I'm not the biggest kiwi fan – but I know that they're a great source of vitamin C. The healthiest way to eat a kiwi is of course just as it is – try slicing in half and serving in egg cups so your child can scoop out the flesh with a teaspoon. The icing really enhances the flavours of these cupcakes. They're best eaten on the same day you make them simply because the cream cheese shouldn't be left out unrefrigerated for too long – and if you bung the cakes with icing in the refrigerator, they'll dry out after a while. So yes, I'm giving you permission to scoff them all in one day!

COOKERY SKILLS: I CAN PRACTISE PEELING FRUIT AND ICING CUPCAKES

SHOPPING LIST

For the cupcakes:

2 eggs

2 ripe kiwi fruit

125 g (4 oz) soft butter or margarine

150 g (5 oz) caster sugar

Juice of 1 lime

½ tsp lime zest

150 g (5 oz) self-raising flour

150 ml (¼ pint) soured cream

For the cream cheese lime icing:

100 g (3½ oz) cream cheese

30 g (1 oz) sifted icing sugar

1 tsp fresh lime juice (pinch a bit from the lime above)

MAKES 12

APRONS ON, LET'S COOK!

1 Preheat the oven to 170°C/325°F/gas 3. Ask a child to place 12 paper muffin cases in a muffin tray.

2 Gently whisk the eggs – or ask your child to (they could also have a go at breaking the eggs into the bowl with supervision).

3 Peel the kiwi fruit, slice and then chop into small pieces – your child can help with this too (and the following mixing). Using a fork, cream the butter or margarine and sugar until it's soft and reasonably fluffy (a few minutes). Add the eggs. It may curdle, but don't panic. Stir through the lime juice and zest too.

4 Sift in the flour and stir through gently. Add the soured cream. Stir all – again, gently – to combine.

5 Divide between the paper cases. Place in the preheated oven for 18–22 minutes until golden brown and firm. Keep checking towards the end to allow for oven variations.

6 Leave the cupcakes in their tin on top of the oven for a good 10 minutes. Then leave to cool completely on a wire rack.

7 Once cool, make the icing: using a fork, whip up the cream cheese to soften it a bit. Add the sugar and lime juice and stir through. Using a blunt butter knife (or similar) slather the icing on top.

GOURMET FOR GROWN-UPS

Simply go for a more sophisticated topping such as lime zest or a few kiwi slices, strategically layered!

exotic fruit

MARKETING EXOTIC FRUIT

I love the taste of tropical fruits but admit they can come in funny shapes and sizes, with names that are funnier still (kumquats anyone?!). I'd always start with the sweeter varieties (mango, papaya or guava) and move on to the more unusual. With the more unusual varieties (passion fruit, pomegranate and lychees spring to mind), explore the shapes and textures together, inviting your child to sample just a little. Perhaps place a piece of the fruit on a plate and say to your child – with a smile – that you could both try the fruit at the exact same time, '5, 4, 3, 2, 1 – GO!' Then give marks out of 10 on a score-sheet (this is a handy technique you can employ for other foods too).

TRY THIS...

A really nice combination, believe it or not, is chicken and mango. Try skewering alternate pieces of cooked, char-grilled chicken with chunks of fresh, juicy mango. Another idea is to simply whizz up soft, tropical fruits to a purée and serve as 'sauce' to stir through a bowl of plain yogurt. Finally, one of my all-time most successful sandwich-filler ideas (and one that nearly all my mum-friends have pinched) has been cream cheese and blueberries.

TROPICAL CLAFOUTIS

This is actually somewhere between a clafoutis and bread-and-butter pudding – Caribbean style! Do make sure you don't over-beat the batter mix or you risk a chewy, tough dessert. Be careful, by the way, the pineapple does retain a lot of heat and takes a while to cool down.

COOKERY SKILLS: I CAN LEARN HOW MERINGUE IS MADE

SHOPPING LIST

30 g (1 oz) unsalted butter, melted, plus extra for greasing

1 medium–large ripe banana

1 x 432-g (15-oz) tin pineapple chunks in juice, drained, or 300 g (10 oz) fresh pineapple

60 g (2½ oz) flour with a pinch of salt

80 g (3 oz) caster sugar

40 g (1½ oz) desiccated coconut

2 eggs, separated

1 tsp vanilla extract

150 ml (¼ pint) whole milk (or 50/50 milk and cream)

SERVES 6

APRONS ON, LET'S COOK!

1 Preheat the oven to 170°C/325°F/gas 3. Generously grease a medium-sized ovenproof baking dish with some butter.

2 With a plastic knife, get your child to slice the banana and place into the dish. They could also have a go at slicing the pineapple chunks a bit smaller and again, placing them in the dish.

3 Sift together the flour and salt into a bowl. Add the sugar and coconut and gently stir to combine.

4 Whisk the egg yolks, melted butter and vanilla extract into the milk in a separate bowl.

5 Whisk the egg whites until they form soft peaks (this is best done with an electric whisk or food processor with a whisk attachment).

6 Meanwhile, gently combine the milk mixture with the dry ingredients. Very gently add the egg whites to this mixture, stirring gently as you go.

7 Pour this batter over the fruit and place in the preheated oven for around 30 minutes, until the top is golden and risen. Leave to cool slightly before serving. This is delicious served with good-quality vanilla ice cream – or even my avocado ice cream (see page 57).

GOURMET FOR GROWN-UPS

Add more tropical fruits, such as chopped mango and papaya – and perhaps a good dash of Malibu to the batter mix.

COCONUT CREAM ICE LOLLIES

This is an all-time favourite of mine – so simple and yet a real crowd-pleaser. They really remind me of the 'milk' lollies I used to enjoy as a kid – and yet these are far more natural, and cheaper to boot. You will need ice lolly moulds – or DIY your own – for this recipe.

COOKERY SKILLS: I CAN SCRAPE SEEDS FROM A VANILLA POD

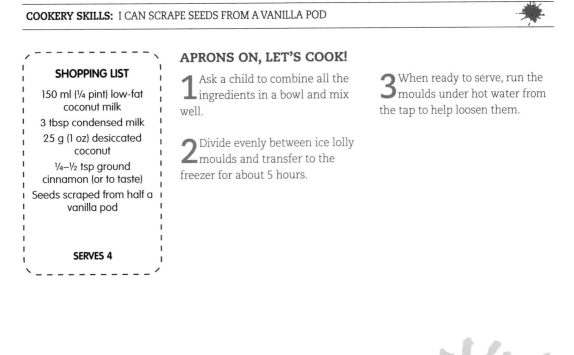

SHOPPING LIST

150 ml (¼ pint) low-fat coconut milk

3 tbsp condensed milk

25 g (1 oz) desiccated coconut

¼–½ tsp ground cinnamon (or to taste)

Seeds scraped from half a vanilla pod

SERVES 4

APRONS ON, LET'S COOK!

1 Ask a child to combine all the ingredients in a bowl and mix well.

2 Divide evenly between ice lolly moulds and transfer to the freezer for about 5 hours.

3 When ready to serve, run the moulds under hot water from the tap to help loosen them.

NOTE
Try using coconut flavoured Greek yoghurt – and blending with a little mango puree. Then simply pour into moulds.

GOURMET FOR GROWN-UPS

Add tiny pineapple chunks for Piña Colada style lollies!

breakfast

MARKETING BREAKFAST

I'm actually more concerned here with how breakfast cereals are marketed to kids by the advertisers. Many breakfast cereals are loaded with hidden salts and sugars. And what makes it harder for parents is that the nutritional info on the side of cereal boxes (even those 'cartoony cereals' clearly aimed at kids) are recommended levels of sugar and salt for adults, not kids. I've researched around a lot and far and away the healthiest cereal option for children is good old-fashioned porridge oats (or something like Ready Brek). Try serving it with mashed banana or agave syrup to sweeten naturally. Although a little spoonful of sugar wouldn't do any harm either.

TRY THIS...

Having said all of the above, I also know that busy families often need quick and easy breakfast ideas – and a bit of variety besides porridge oats! As a family we have a little rule that mum decides on breakfast Monday to Friday and at the weekend they can choose other cereals. How about you also occasionally whip up some pancakes – or even create a 'breakfast' pizza – with bacon and a baked egg.

With regard to smoothies, can I also suggest – if your kids are old enough – that you make up a big batch and decant into paper cups with lids and straws (coffee house take-out style) – great for particularly busy mornings. The following is a bit self-indulgent but is our all-time favourite smoothie recipe.

Banana Peanut Butter Smoothie:
2 ripe bananas
2 tbsp peanut butter (crunchy or smooth)
4 tbsp natural yogurt
100 ml (3½ fl oz) semi-skimmed or whole milk
1–2 tsp agave syrup (or runny honey)

Simply whizz up in a blender or smoothie maker and serve.

STRAWBERRY AND BANANA BREAKFAST MILKSHAKE

I'm calling this 'milkshake' not just for the marketing factor but also because it has the look and texture of a milkshake. I know I've been a bit pedantic with the 'ripe' bananas and 'at room temperature' strawberries – I just think that these things do make a big difference. (Just as I'm fanatical about keeping tomatoes out of the fridge, I feel the same about strawberries…) The agave syrup gives less of a sugar energy 'spike' than honey or other sugars and is entirely natural. You'll need a smoothie maker, blender or similar for this recipe.

COOKERY SKILLS: I CAN PRACTISE CHOPPING FRUIT

SHOPPING LIST

1 medium–large ripe banana

10 medium–large ripe strawberries, hulled and at room temperature

1 tsp agave syrup (or runny honey)

3 tbsp Ready Brek or porridge oats

2 tbsp natural, live yogurt

100 ml (3½ fl oz) milk

SERVES 4 KIDS

APRONS ON, LET'S COOK!

1 I find that it helps to break up the banana and strawberries a bit before putting in the blender – this is a perfect job for little ones to do with a plastic knife (they can even mush it all down a bit with a fork or spoon or their hands).

2 Put all the ingredients in the blender and whizz up until pink and smooth.

GOURMET FOR GROWN-UPS

Any gym-bunnies out there? This is a great pre-/post-workout smoothie. Try adding some ground flaxseed for added omega oils.

PINK PORRIDGE

With two daughters, pink is a very big deal in our house. Needless to say, this one sort of sells itself. You will need a blender or food processor for this recipe.

COOKERY SKILLS: I CAN PRACTISE STIRRING CAREFULLY

APRONS ON, LET'S COOK!

1 Place the apple, sugar, water and cinnamon in a saucepan and cook over a medium heat for 3 minutes, stirring occasionally.

2 Add the strawberries and raspberries and cook for a further 3 minutes or so – until the apple is soft (everything will cook quicker if you place a lid on the saucepan). This may be a good opportunity for an older child to help stir, under careful supervision.

3 Pour it all into a blender or food processor and whizz up until smooth.

4 Return the blitzed mixture to the saucepan and add the oats and milk. Cook over a low heat for about 5 minutes, until the porridge oats have softened, stirring all the time.

5 Serve immediately, perhaps topping with more berries, flaked almonds, a seed mix or yogurt.

NOTE
For me it makes sense to have a filling meal at the start of the day – and gradually eat less as the evening draws in so I always make a big batch of this so Matt and I can have some too!

GOURMET FOR GROWN-UPS

If you have guests staying over, the blended fruit makes a lovely compote to serve at breakfast with some Greek yogurt.

slimy foods
(aubergine and mushrooms)

MARKETING AUBERGINES AND MUSHROOMS

You may wonder why these are in the same category. It's really because (in my experience and as the food title suggests) kids often reject both of these vegetables for their texture alone. And these two don't have entirely dissimilar textures as well as very distinctive tastes.

They're tricky ones to market but are also ideally suited to get older kids to practice their knife skills (which may go a long way in marketability). Supervise as they hold the vegetables steady (stalks off for mushrooms) and slice through, ready for cooking. I also like to refer to mushrooms as baby umbrellas. Get your kids to look at the underside and stroke the soft, brown texture.

TRY THIS...

Try finely chopping mushrooms, stir-frying in a little butter and garlic and adding to grated cheese. Then place this on sliced bread and grill it until the cheese has melted – mushroom rarebit. Or try stuffing large mushrooms with the stuffed tomato filling on page 26.

MUSHROOM AND HALLOUMI SKEWERS

The halloumi is almost the star of the show here – but that's ok because it renders the mushrooms suddenly rather conventional. The mushrooms are cooked until just *al dente*. If your child falls in love with the halloumi (as many do as don't), you could try stuffing the innards of a mushroom with it (remove the stalk). By all means grill these but they're crying out to be barbecued too. You will need wooden skewers for this recipe.

COOKERY SKILLS: I CAN LEARN HOW TO SKEWER FOOD BY MAKING VEGETABLE KEBABS

SHOPPING LIST

200–300 g (7–8 oz) new baby potatoes, quartered.

25 g (1 oz) unsalted butter

½–1 garlic clove, crushed

150 g (5 oz) button mushrooms, gently washed and dried

250 g (8 oz) halloumi cheese, chopped into chunks (a bit smaller than the mushrooms)

Salt

SERVES 4–6

APRONS ON, LET'S COOK!

1 Soak the wooden skewers in cold water for about 30 minutes to prevent them burning.

2 Cover the potatoes with boiled water in a large saucepan, add a pinch of salt, and cook on a rapid simmer for about 15 minutes (you want them cooked but not too soft and crumbly).

3 Meanwhile, melt the butter in a separate pan and add the garlic and the mushrooms. Sauté until the mushrooms are just cooked – not too soft and still with some shape and texture.

4 Place the sautéed mushrooms in a large bowl (pouring in the buttery garlic juices) and add the cooked, drained potatoes. Very gently mix – just to give the potatoes a bit of a coating. Preheat the grill to a medium setting.

5 Skewer alternate pieces of potato, mushroom and halloumi – perhaps two of each. Perhaps a child could help with this under careful supervision. Place the skewers under the grill for about 10 minutes, turning occasionally (don't worry – the halloumi keeps its shape and won't drip).

GOURMET FOR GROWN-UPS

These look sooooo pretty – and add a gorgeous smokiness – when skewered onto bald sprigs of rosemary – keep some rosemary at the top for aesthetic reasons (although you do need to ensure the sprigs don't burn).

AUBERGINE CRISPIES

I know that this isn't the most elegant of aubergine dishes and frying in oil isn't the healthiest thing to do but do remember that the point of this book is to persuade your kids to try certain foods – and this is simply the recipe I've had the biggest success rate with when it comes to aubergine.

Don't be tempted to make the batter in advance and remember that the water needs to be as cold as possible so use water straight from the fridge. Likewise keep an eye on the oil – it needs to be very hot – but not so hot that the tempura burns almost within moments of touching the oil. Please do take care with the frying pan of hot oil – the consequences of such scalding hot oil on their skin (or yours) is unthinkable. Once you're done with the oil, remember to let it cool down fully (at the back of the hob) before discarding – in the bin, not the sink!

COOKERY SKILLS: I CAN LEARN HOW TO GENTLY STIR AND COMBINE

SHOPPING LIST

100 g (3½ oz) self-raising flour

½ tsp salt

Just over 100 ml (3½ oz) cold sparkling water (you will need 100 ml plus an extra tbsp or so)

2 baby aubergines, cut into slices about 5 mm (¼ in) thick

Vegetable or sunflower oil (about 750 ml (1¼ pints) or enough to fill a large frying pan about half way up)

SERVES 6–8

NOTE
This recipe is not suitable for under-threes as it exceeds their recommended daily allowance of salt.

APRONS ON, LET'S COOK!

1 Put the flour and salt into a mixing bowl. Add the water and whisk gently with a fork to create a very thick batter. Try not to over mix it. A child could do this job – remind them to be 'gentle'. Older kids could chop the aubergine, if you and they are confident of their knife skills.

2 At this stage I would ensure that younger kids are set up on a different activity. It's rare I shoo kids out of the kitchen – but this is one of those exceptions (see safety note above). Older kids could help with covering the aubergine in the batter – see Step 4.

3 Pour enough of the oil in a frying pan so it comes to half way up the sides. Slowly heat it up so it's very hot (a small piece of bread should sizzle when dropped into it). If you feel like using a cook's thermometer, the temperature should be about 180°C/350°F. Don't heat it up too quickly or have on too high a heat or the tempura will burn. Equally it needs to be a good strong heat. Whatever you do, please keep the pan at the back of the hob (again, just for safety).

4 Place pieces of aubergine in the batter so both sides are coated then place on a large metal spoon to lower into the hot oil. Let the tempura cook for a 1–2 minutes until just pale golden. If it goes very golden brown within a minute then your heat is too high so adjust it slightly.

5 Remove, carefully, with a slotted spoon and allow to drain and cool slightly on a plate with some kitchen roll.

6 Serve with dips – yogurt and mint works well – or some sweet chilli dipping sauce if you think it will go down well.

deli foods

MARKETING DELI FOODS

My best tip? Go to a deli! Not only is it lovely to support them, but they're also very likely to invite (or allow) your child to sample a few of the goods. One fantastic game you can play is the Roll The Dice Tapas Game: simply have six little deli dishes on the table, numbered 1–6, roll the dice and see what number comes up – whatever the number is, this is the dish you have to eat. Keep it fun and with a wide range of flavours – including a sweet one to keep your children interested.

TRY THIS...

My husband in particular loves the Spanish way of eating. Spanish tapas are lots of little dishes with loads of different flavours. Re-create the same at home with a mini kids' tapas bar. Pretend it's a restaurant, café or a deli (with pretend money). You could also create artichoke crisps, as described with potatoes on page 52. I've also had a few takers when I've (painstakingly) cut out mini stars shapes from banana slices and dipped them in fresh beetroot juice – pink banana stars!

SAVOURY OLIVE LOAF

This is adapted from a recipe by the wonderful Mary Cadogan. As a journalist I once reviewed one of Mary's cookery classes at her beautiful home in south-west France and was hugely impressed by all the local produce and flavours (along with Mary's use of these in her recipes). Do look her up if you're ever in the area. Sounds obvious but do make sure the olives are stoned. This is a great picnic recipe – wrap in foil soon after the loaf is out of the oven and it'll still be warm and moist when you arrive and unpack. Don't forget to take a bread knife and some butter on your picnic though (perhaps try some garlic butter). You'll need a blender or food processor for this recipe.

COOKERY SKILLS: I CAN PRACTISE WHISKING EGGS AND SIFTING FLOUR

SHOPPING LIST

90–100 g (3½ oz) green olives, pitted

200 g (7 oz) self raising flour, seasoned

3 eggs, beaten

100 ml (3½ fl oz) milk

100 ml (3½ fl oz) olive oil

100 g (3½ oz) grated hard cheese, such as Cheddar

SERVES 6

APRONS ON, LET'S COOK!

1 Preheat the oven to 190°C/375°F/gas 5. Grease and line a 1.2 litre (2 pint) loaf tin.

2 Roughly chop the olives (or whizz them up in the blender or food processor – don't let them get too small though).

3 Whisk the eggs – or ask your child to help.

4 Sift the flour into a large bowl (letting your child/ren help if they want).

5 Add the beaten eggs, milk and oil to the flour and stir to combine. Stir in the chopped olives and two-thirds of the cheese. It should be a nice smooth batter.

6 Pour the mixture into the prepared tin and sprinkle with the remaining cheese. Bake in the preheated oven for about 30–35 minutes until firm and golden and crusty on top. Leave it to rest in the tin for about 5–10 minutes then turn out to cool on a wire rack.

7 Slice and serve slathered with butter.

GOURMET FOR GROWN-UPS

I think here we should revisit Mary's original recipe: add to the mix some steamed or boiled green beans (I'd say around 150–200 g (5–7 oz); 100 g (3½ oz) sun-dried tomatoes, 1 tbsp fresh thyme leaves and some grated hard cheese of your choice (Mary uses Comte).

MEDITERRANEAN MAC AND CHEESE

This recipe is basically macaroni cheese, stepped up a notch. Ensure you add the milk straight from the fridge (cold) to help the sauce stay lump-free. You will need a blender or food processor for this recipe.

COOKERY SKILLS: I CAN PRACTICE CHOPPING VEGETABLES

SHOPPING LIST

About 300 g (10 oz) dried macaroni

75 g (3 oz) sun-blush tomatoes

75 g (3 oz) marinated artichokes

500 ml (17 fl oz) whole milk

50 g (2 oz) unsalted butter

50 g (2 oz) flour, sifted

110 g (3½ oz) grated hard cheese, such as Cheddar

Black pepper

SERVES 2 ADULTS, PLUS 2–4 KIDS

APRONS ON, LET'S COOK!

1 Cook the macaroni according to the packet instructions.

2 Drain any excess oil from the tomatoes and artichokes and invite your child to help you chop them up (it doesn't matter if this is very roughly).

3 Whizz the tomatoes and artichokes in a blender or food processor. Next time you could leave them chunkier if your child seems to like the flavours.

4 Put the milk, butter and flour in a medium–large saucepan over a medium–high heat and simply keep whisking until the sauce thickens. Once it has thickened, add a twist of black pepper, add the cheese and stir until it melts.

5 Add the tomatoes and artichokes and stir through, along with the (cooked and drained) macaroni. Serve immediately.

GOURMET FOR GROWN-UPS

Add a pinch of cayenne pepper (or paprika or nutmeg) to the cheese sauce. You could also add diced olives and fish or meat of any description (salmon perhaps?) and serve topped with breadcrumbs and sliced tomatoes.

herbs, spices and stronger flavours

MARKETING HERBS AND SPICES

One of the easiest ways to get your kids into herbs is by growing them yourself. I don't have particularly green fingers but even I can keep our basil plant alive. Plus of course by their very nature, herbs can get your kids used to the dreaded 'green' foods. Spices can be a little trickier as, again by nature, they're stronger to taste – but Elsie, my youngest daughter, has

> **"**From a dad's perspective, Fiona gave us a few recipes that we could also go home and impress our other halves with. I still miss those Saturday morning classes!**"**
>
> **Martin Humphries**

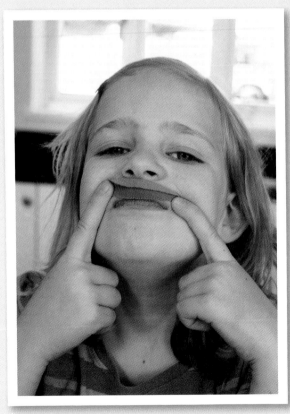

killed many a happy half an hour simply re-organising my little spice pots, asking me what each one is called and us discussing their colours and (carefully) smelling them.

TRY THIS...

If your kids like eggs, try adding a few chopped fresh herbs to an omelette – or even chopped fresh parsley sprinkled on top of cheese on toast. Don't forget that both cinnamon and nutmeg are spices so don't be afraid to use these in savoury dishes, such as cheese sauces. Another simple idea is to slice a bread muffin in half, rub with a peeled garlic clove, then spread with butter and toast in the oven.

BAKED SPICED TORTILLA CHIPS

These are an ideal accompaniment to Hummus in a Hurry (see page 44) – and also a great after-school snack. Play around with the spice quantities to suit your child's palate: ¼ teaspoon isn't enough for Darcey (who is a bit of a spice-monkey), ½ teaspoon is way-overload for Finn! I'd definitely start with the ¼ teaspoon and see how you all go.

COOKERY SKILLS: I CAN PRACTISE USING A PASTRY BRUSH

SHOPPING LIST

2 tbsp olive oil
¼–½ tsp cayenne pepper
(or ¼ tsp cayenne and
¼ tsp ground nutmeg)
2 (soft) flour tortillas
(preferably organic)

SERVES 4–6

APRONS ON, LET'S COOK!

1 Preheat the oven to 220°C/425°F/gas 7.

2 Get your child to whisk together the oil and spice(s) in a small bowl.

3 Place the wraps one on top of the other and with kitchen scissors cut into halves, then quarters, then eighths – so you have 16 triangle shapes. Older kids could do the cutting whilst supervised.

4 Place the triangles on a baking tray (either 2 or 1 big one) and ask a child to brush each shape with the oil-spice mix on both sides.

5 Bake for about 4–5 minutes until crispy and golden. Leave to firm up a bit on the baking tray, then place on a plate with kitchen towel to cool and drain off any excess oil.

NOTE
These are a good addition to kids' lunch boxes – a perfect alternative to salty crisps.

GOURMET FOR GROWN-UPS

If I'm making these for me and my husband, I always add a sprinkling of chilli flakes too.

PARSLEY CHAMP

This recipe uses an old favourite – mashed potato – as a 'safe' carrier for slightly stronger flavours. The kids will love the mish-mashing part of this recipe (never put potatoes in a blender as it makes them all gluey) and they can also get involved in tearing up the parsley – or even choosing the variety ('flat-leaf or curly?') This recipe is also a nice introduction to onion (it uses the milder spring onion variety – these are cooked in a little milk to further dilute their strength and make them a little more palatable for kids).

COOKERY SKILLS: I CAN PRACTISE MASHING POTATO AND TEARING UP HERBS

SHOPPING LIST

About 500 g (1 lb) potatoes, peeled and chopped

A couple of spring onions, finely chopped

150 ml (¼ pint) milk

75 g (3 oz) frozen peas (optional)

25 g (1 oz) unsalted butter

1 tbsp crème fraîche

1 tbsp freshly chopped or torn parsley

A pinch of salt

SERVES 4

APRONS ON, LET'S COOK!

1 Place the chopped potatoes in a saucepan, cover with water and boil until tender – this should take 15–20 minutes.

2 Once the potatoes have been boiling for 10–15 minutes, put the onions, milk and peas (if using) in a small saucepan and bring to a simmer. Cook for a couple of minutes.

3 Once the potatoes are cooked, drain them, return to the pan, add the butter, and mash. Maybe your child/ren could help with this (under careful supervision as the pan will still be hot). They could also help to add the milk, onion and peas (if using) as well as the crème fraîche and mash again.

4 Stir through the parsley and season to taste with salt (not too much). Serve immediately. This mash goes especially well with fish fingers.

GOURMET FOR GROWN-UPS

Bake up some jacket potatoes, scoop out the flesh and use in the recipe for champ before spooning back into the hollow potato skins. Top with a little feta cheese and serve with grilled fish.

meat

MARKETING MEAT

In my experience kids are either carnivorous, or not, so it may be that you have a natural 'veggie' on your hands (as I think I do with Elsie). But I do think that a lot of kids (fans of meat or not) have issues with its texture. If they have to chew it for ages, it really can put them off. Fatty, grisly meat doesn't usually go down well either. Focus on small, lean and tender cuts of meat and remember, smaller tummies need smaller portion sizes. Many parents have tried the 'here comes the aeroplane' technique with the fork. How about going a step further and transforming your child's fork or spoon into other modes of transportation: a sports car; daddy's van; or a princess carriage.

TRY THIS...

I'm not a fan of hiding meat in sauces where kids are clearly against the idea of eating meat (or certain meats). That just doesn't sit right with me. But if meat is an issue with your child and you think it's based more on texture than taste, then perhaps try serving up some good-quality ham, thinly sliced and diced, onto a tasty pizza and see how you go. You could also create a calzone 'pizza pocket' so the meat is tasted but doesn't create an obvious 'visual'. Or create veggie sausages or burgers and slowly add or introduce a little meat into the recipe mix (such as finely shredded chicken).

Your chicken sausages were a big hit – please can I have the recipe?!

Shauna Emsley, mum to Caitlin (aged 6)

CARAMELIZED PEAR PUFFS WITH GOATS' CHEESE AND BACON

So here's the deal: yes, these are a little time-consuming – not excessively so, but equally not a 'knock em up in 5 minutes job'. The point is however – as with all my recipes – that kids should just love the end result and enjoy getting involved with actually making them. These are super-cute and tasty! Two things though: firstly, please do roll the pastry out really thin and roll in straight lines so as not to disturb the layers; secondly, ensure the sides are all even and square, so it's easy to fold into a rectangle. Oh, and thirdly, don't make them too big – try to stick to my measurements.

COOKERY SKILLS: I CAN PRACTISE ROLLING OUT PASTRY AND GREASING BAKING TRAYS

SHOPPING LIST

About 6 good-quality bacon rashers

Flour, for dusting

1 x 500 g (1 lb) pack of ready-to-roll puff pastry, at room temperature

1 pear

1 tsp butter

1 tsp sugar

About 50 g (2 oz) goats' cheese

1 egg, beaten

MAKES ABOUT 15 MINI PARCELS

GOURMET FOR GROWN-UPS

Play around with the fillings here: creamy blue cheese, chopped walnuts and pear is lovely – ditto cheddar, ham and pesto… keep them small and serve warm with a leafy green salad and bottle of something chilled – the perfect lunch!

APRONS ON, LET'S COOK!

1 Preheat the oven to 200°C/400°F/gas 6. Meanwhile grill the bacon until it's just pink – not crispy. When the bacon is cooked, cover and set aside.

2 Lightly flour a large, clean surface. Unwrap the puff pastry and slice the block firmly into four quarters, using nice, straight lines. Take one quarter and, using a rolling pin, roll it as thin as you can (we're talking about 1 mm here) in as square a shape as you can. What you're looking to do is to create lots of little square shapes – about 8 cm x 8 cm (3 ½ in x 3 ½ in). The sides need to be straight and even, so use a ruler if you can – the idea is to fold them into perfect little triangles.

3 Leave your squares to one side for a moment (don't stack them) and peel and quarter the pear, using a teaspoon to scoop out the core. Chop into smallish pieces.

4 Melt the butter in a pan, add the sugar and pear and simmer for about 3 minutes. Set aside and leave to cool in the sugary butter.

5 Using scissors, cut away all the fat and rind from the bacon and then cut into little pieces. Set aside.

6 Return to the pear and chop it into similar-sized pieces as the bacon. Set aside. Ask a child to grease a baking tray.

7 Take a square of pastry and ask your child if they'd like to dip their finger into the beaten egg and run it around the edge of the square.

8 Load up the centre of the squares with tiny portions of chopped pear, bacon and a dab of goats' cheese. Fold one corner over the other, creating a triangle shape. Pick it up and secure the edges with your thumb and forefinger. Again, ask your child to run a little of the beaten egg over the top of the triangle parcel. Repeat and put each finished triangle onto the greased baking tray.

9 Bake in the preheated oven for about 10 minutes until crisp and golden.

CHICKEN AND PARMESAN SECRET SAUSAGES

As I said, my youngest daughter isn't the biggest meat eater in the world – but even she wolfs these down with gusto every time they're on the menu. They're not as 'sturdy' as regular sausages so treat with a little TLC when cooking. They're a really lovely alternative to the fatty pork ones and even my uber-carnivorous husband likes them. I like to serve these, hot-dog style, with mayo rather than ketchup, in soft wholemeal rolls. I often make these with leftover meat from our Sunday roast. What's the secret? The hidden bit of apple – it adds moisture and a subtle bit of extra flavour. You will need a blender or food processor for this recipe.

COOKERY SKILLS: I CAN LEARN HOW TO MAKE SAUSAGES

SHOPPING LIST

25 g (1 oz) butter

1 small red onion, chopped

1 apple, cored, peeled and cut into chunks (about 100 g (3½ oz))

2 sage leaves (optional – but they give a nice bit of flavour)

200 g (7 oz) cooked diced chicken

25 g (1 oz) finely grated parmesan

60 g (2½ oz) fresh breadcrumbs (whizz up old bread crusts from a loaf – better still, let a small child do the same with their hands and a large bowl)

Oil, for frying

Salt

MAKES 6 SAUSAGES

APRONS ON, LET'S COOK!

1 Melt the butter in a pan over medium-high heat. Add the onion and sauté for a good 3 minutes or so.

2 Add the apple and sage and stir through for another minute.

3 Place the chicken, parmesan and breadcrumbs in a large bowl and add in the contents of the saucepan. Stir to mix everything together.

4 Put it all in a blender or food processor, with a pinch of salt and whizz up until the mixture is finely chopped and thoroughly blended together.

5 With clean, slightly oiled hands, you and your child can create 6 large sausages, or 10 small ones. Transfer these to the fridge for about 30–60 minutes to firm up.

6 When you're ready to cook them, heat up some oil in a non-stick frying pan, and simply heat these through, turning as you go, so each side becomes golden.

GOURMET FOR GROWN-UPS

Serve these as an alternative Boxing Day supper – replacing the chicken with leftover turkey and the addition of some fresh cranberries.

fish

MARKETING FISH

The idea of fish can be very off-putting to some kids so, ideally, start them young and offer lots of cheesy, creamy dishes, such as fisherman's pies. Whether or not you take them to a fishmonger or fresh fish counter is your call. I know as many kids who've loved it as not. Interestingly, my daughter Elsie is not really into the idea of fish – but loves those fresh salmon and cream cheese canapés you can buy. Something in ditching the fishy name? Who knows? Just keep experimenting with ideas and if you fall flat on your face, try and up their intake of other foods with healthy omega oils, such as avocado.

TRY THIS...

How about going retro and introducing your kids to a good old-fashioned prawn cocktail? I've known some fish-haters to love the idea of calamari too. If all else fails, I advise parents to try grilling up some fish fingers and serve fish finger sandwiches with ketchup. It'd be a good start at least.

SMOKED SALMON CRISPY PANCAKES

This recipe does take a little time to prepare – but it's also very simple. You can use pretty much any filling you fancy – I often make it with a cheese sauce and some flaked cod or haddock. You could also replace the fish with pieces of grilled bacon (and again, cheese sauce), or add a bolognaise mix or vegetable ratatouille.

COOKERY SKILLS: I CAN PRACTISE SIFTING FLOUR AND CAREFULLY FILLING PANCAKES

SHOPPING LIST

For the pancakes:
250 g (8 oz) plain flour
¼ tsp salt
2 eggs
500 ml (17 fl oz) milk
Vegetable oil, for frying

For the filling:
300 g (10 oz) cream cheese
125 g (4 oz) smoked salmon

For the coating:
75 g (3 oz) flour seasoned with a small pinch of salt
2 beaten eggs
6 slices of wholemeal bread, whizzed up in a food processor to make breadcrumbs

MAKES 8

GOURMET FOR GROWN-UPS

Add a squeeze of fresh lime juice and some chopped herbs (mint, chives or dill) to the mix. Add a sprinkling of paprika and cayenne pepper to the breadcrumbs to create a bit more of a kick!

APRONS ON, LET'S COOK!

1 First, put a large lidded pan of water on to boil.

2 Get your child to sift the flour and salt into a large bowl. Add the eggs and milk and using a fork or whisk, mix to create the pancake batter. Help them transfer it to a jug so it is easier to pour.

3 To make the filling, your child can whip the cream cheese with a fork so it softens a little. Using scissors, you can snip off tiny shards of salmon into the cream cheese. Mix it all together and set aside.

4 Start making the pancakes. Heat 1 tablespoon of oil in a small frying pan, then pour about 2 tablespoons of batter in. Don't make the pancakes too thin – they need to withstand filling and flipping. Try and keep to a round shape and don't over-cook them. Cook the pancakes on both sides until golden. Transfer to a plate resting on top of the simmering pan of water. Cover the plate (and pancake) with a lid. Keep going like this with all the pancakes, adding more oil to the frying pan where necessary.

5 Once you've cooked up all the pancakes, you can start to fill them. Put 1 tablespoon of filling in one half of the pancake circle. Using a dab of batter on your finger create a 'glue' by tracing around one half of the pancake edge then fold over the other half – so it's a semi-circular, half-moon shape.

6 Once all the pancakes have been filled, create a work station for the coating: a bowl of seasoned flour, a bowl of whisked egg and a bowl of breadcrumbs. Carefully dip each filled pancake into the flour, then coat in some of the egg and finally plunge into the breadcrumbs.

7 Heat up a good glug of vegetable oil in the same little frying pan and carefully add a pancake to the pan with a spatula. Fry off on both sides until golden, draining on a plate with a piece of kitchen towel as you cook in batches. They can be tricky to flip over so use a pair of tongs. Serve once slightly cooled.

MEATBALLS WITH A TWIST

This idea was originally inspired by a Jamie Oliver recipe (one of my all-time culinary heroes). If you're a busy parent – keep it simple and don't beat yourself up for using pasta sauce from a jar. By the way, these freeze really well – plus can be served cold as a snack (once cooked and cooled down) or chopped into a wholemeal pitta bread with a bit of mayo and tomato – instant healthy packed lunch.

COOKERY SKILLS: I CAN LEARN HOW TO CREATE MEATBALLS

SHOPPING LIST

2 tbsp olive oil

1 small onion, very finely chopped

1 garlic clove, finely chopped

75 g (3 oz) pine nuts, whizzed in a blender or food processor until they're like breadcrumbs

2 x 185 g (6½ oz) tins tuna in spring water

Juice of 1 lime

1 egg, beaten

140 g (4½ oz) fresh breadcrumbs

A small handful of fresh parsley, finely chopped

Cooked spaghetti or pasta and some tomato pasta sauce, to serve

Salt and pepper

**MAKES ABOUT
25 MEATBALLS**

APRONS ON, LET'S COOK!

1 Melt the oil in in a frying pan. Add the onion, garlic and pine nuts and sauté for 1–2 minutes over a medium–high heat. Set aside.

2 Drain the tuna and, with a fork, flake it into a large mixing bowl (a perfect job for kids). Also get the kids to help with adding the lime juice, egg, breadcrumbs and parsley. Mix thoroughly with a metal spoon.

3 Add in the onion, garlic and pine nuts and mix again. Add a small pinch of salt and pepper.

4 Take small handfuls of the mixture, squeeze into little equal-sized meatballs (no bigger than a golf ball – about walnut sized) and place on a baking tray as you go. Some kids will love doing this. Others will hate the idea of getting so messy. Use your own judgement but don't use pressure. Transfer the meatballs to the fridge for an hour or so to let them firm up a bit.

5 Heat another glug of oil in a non-stick frying pan and fry the meatballs over a medium–high heat until golden brown and heated through. Serve with pasta and fresh tomato pasta sauce along with extra sprinklings of fresh parsley.

GOURMET FOR GROWN-UPS

Obviously for starters you could impress by making your own pasta sauce (and pasta) – or simply add in more veggies (grated carrot, sweetcorn, baby broccoli florets). Either way, serve the meatballs in a big dish: spaghetti, then sauce, then meatballs, topped with fresh, chopped parsley – it looks so pretty and summery.

eggs and brown bread

MARKETING EGGS AND BROWN BREAD

Eggs can be fun as a PR exercise: take your kids to see some chickens and explain how they lay fresh eggs for us. In fact, why not rescue some battery hens and keep your own? As for brown bread (and by brown I mean wholemeal), why not play up to its different colour by creating sandwiches with one slice of brown and one of white as a good starting point.

TRY THIS...

How about creating a Fiorentina pizza recipe with a baked egg in the middle? Or just keep things simple: hard-boil an egg, allow to cool, mash with some mayo and use as a sandwich filler. Equally, if you don't have an issue with raw egg – and are not pregnant – older kids may enjoy making egg nog.

SOMERSET EGGS

This is my take on Scotch eggs (so-called because of the inclusion of apple – and here in Somerset, we're renowned for our fantastic apple orchards). These end up much bigger than standard shop-bought Scotch eggs – one could be split between two kids quite easily – though Finn adores these and could probably hoover down a whole batch! This recipe is almost interchangeable with the Meat chapter; if your kids aren't sure about eggs but love sausages, try this! Again, if your kids aren't sure about meat but love eggs, try this! Either way, be sure to buy the best quality sausages you can afford.

COOKERY SKILLS: I CAN PEEL HARD-BOILED EGGS

SHOPPING LIST

4 eggs, plus 1 further egg, beaten

4 good-quality sausages (or 6 chipolatas)

1 apple, peeled and grated

Salt and pepper

Pinch of garlic granules (optional)

1 crust of wholemeal bread, whizzed up to make breadcrumbs

50 g (2 oz) plain flour, lightly seasoned

Oil, for frying

MAKES 4

GOURMET FOR GROWN-UPS

Serve halved, sprinkled with chopped chives and a dollop of garlic mayonnaise on the side.

APRONS ON, LET'S COOK!

1 Put four of the eggs in a pan, cover with water, bring to the boil and simmer for a good 8 minutes so they're hard-boiled. Drain and then immerse in cold water to cool down before carefully peeling each egg. Older kids can help with the peeling.

2 Slit the sausages lengthways with a sharp knife and slide the sausage meat out of the skins. Place the meat in a bowl with the grated apple. Season the mix (if you want, add some garlic granules too, but just a pinch) and mix thoroughly with a metal spoon.

3 Divide the mix into four equal portions and pat down into oval shapes about 10 cm (5 in) long by about 8 cm (3½ in) wide. Remember to wash hands and surfaces after handling raw meat.

4 Carefully cover each hard-boiled egg with a coating of the apple-sausage mix so each egg is thoroughly covered.

5 Start to heat up a small saucepan of oil over a medium heat – enough so that each egg can be immersed. You don't want it overly hot so the eggs burn. Equally you need it hot enough to cook them. As a test, drop in a small bit of bread. If it quickly sizzles, the oil is ready. Keep any kids away from the hot oil.

6 Set up a little work station of a bowl of flour, a bowl of beaten egg and a bowl of breadcrumbs. Dip the eggs firstly in the flour, then egg and then the breadcrumbs. Kids can definitely help here.

7 Fry each egg (using a slotted spoon) for about 5 minutes. Leave to cool, draining on a plate covered with kitchen towel. Make sure you cut one open to double-check that the sausage meat has cooked through and isn't pink before serving.

SCRAMBLED EGG CUPCAKE STARS

It was a proud day when I created this recipe – and who can resist a cupcake? Yes, essentially this is an extra special scrambled eggs on toast. It is slightly fiddly to make, but all it takes is a bit of extra time. The goats' cheese adds to the flavour and creaminess and you could add almost anything else you wanted (such as bits of bacon, salmon, spring onion, spinach, pineapple chunks). I sometimes make this on a Saturday morning, in the summer when it's warm, and bung them out in the garden with the kids – a hand-held cooked breakfast! This is a good recipe for 'Brown Bread Haters' too.

COOKERY SKILLS: I CAN LEARN HOW TO MAKE PERFECT SCRAMBLED EGGS

SHOPPING LIST

5 slices of wholemeal bread, crusts removed (but don't discard)

1 tsp butter, plus extra for buttering

2 eggs

1 tbsp single cream

25 g (1 oz) goats' cheese, crumbled

Salt and pepper

MAKES 5

GOURMET FOR GROWN-UPS

Create a variety of these and serve on a breakfast platter – some with the breadcrumb topping, some without, some with a swirl of crème fraîche and a lick of salmon, some with criss-cross chives – you could even pipe some cream cheese with an icing nozzle if you wanted to get really fancy.

APRONS ON, LET'S COOK!

1 Preheat the oven to 220°C/425°F/gas 7.

2 Using a rolling pin, roll each slice of bread flat – or ask a child to. Then cut off the lower end to make an equal square. Ask a child to butter one side of each and cut diagonally across so you have two equal triangles.

3 Press the first triangle (butter side down) into one side of a muffin tray mould so the corners face out – do the same with the other triangle but on the opposite side – so effectively you have a star-shaped basket.

4 Do all five and place in the preheated oven for about 7 minutes, until golden and crisped up a bit. Remove from the muffin tray and set aside.

5 Meanwhile, make the scrambled egg. Melt the butter in a small saucepan. Add the eggs, seasoning and cream and whisk over a medium heat (not too high). When you can see that the eggs are about 75 per cent scrambled, take off the heat and add in the goats' cheese – keep whisking, whisking, whisking all the time. Keep explaining what you're doing with the kids as you go.

6 Place about 2 teaspoons of scrambled egg in each star basket and return to the oven for about 2–4 minutes (keep an eye on them to prevent over-cooking). You can serve them like this or maybe create a funny face with vegetables. Alternatively, mine and my kids' favourite way is to take it one step further:

7 Whizz up those bread crusts until they're breadcrumbs, heat a little butter in a pan and sauté the breadcrumbs with a pinch of sea salt until they're crispy (1–2 minutes). Use these as a sprinkle topping for the eggs – delicious!

rice and grains

MARKETING RICE AND GRAINS

Sadly rice and grains aren't as pre-disposed for Toddler Chef 'marketability' as many other foods are. One of my favourite ways of getting kids to handle things such as rice is to fill up empty plastic bottles or containers with rice, secure with a lid and use them as a musical shaker. You can then have fun decorating these and getting your kids into a bit of rhythm and dance. With the rice pudding recipe given opposite be sure to show your kids the brown rice pre- and post-overnight soaking and stress their magical qualities in 'drinking up' water.

TRY THIS...

I'm a huge fan of risotto (see my parsnip risotto recipe on page 29) and would encourage you to experiment with risotto flavours. Risotto rice, once cooked through, is beautifully soft and creamy. You could also create little arancini balls (from the risotto). With couscous, don't be mistaken that this has to be a savoury food; try cooking it with heated-up fresh fruit juices and serving with berries and Greek yogurt – a healthy lunchbox dessert idea perhaps?

GOLDEN BROWN RICE PUDDING

This is one of those puddings that, as an adult, you promise yourself you'll only have one spoonful and end up dipping in for more throughout the day. I make no apologies for the fact that this is very much in the 'sweet dessert' category so in that respect, not exactly a 'health' food – but for growing kids (particularly those who don't like drinking milk) it's a nice, wholesome dessert. The twist here is that I'm using brown rice rather than pudding rice – loaded with B vitamins and with just a tad more texture. In that respect, it serves as a gentle intro to the idea of eating rice. Just remember to put the rice in a small bowl and top up with cold water the night before – a simple but important part of this recipe. There'd be no harm in serving this cold in little containers as part of a school lunchbox.

COOKERY SKILLS: I CAN LEARN HOW TO GREASE AN OVEN DISH

SHOPPING LIST

185 g (6½ oz) brown rice, soaked overnight in cold water

500 ml (17 fl oz) whole milk

150 ml (¼ pint) single cream

125 g (4 oz) golden caster sugar

¼–½ tsp cinnamon

A pinch of nutmeg

Butter, for greasing

SERVES 6–8

APRONS ON, LET'S COOK!

1 The soaked rice should have absorbed most of the water – and in doing so softened quite substantially. Ask your child to place it all in a large non-stick saucepan. Add all the other ingredients and stir through.

2 Over a gentle heat, bring the rice to a slow boil, stirring regularly. Once it starts to bubble slightly, turn the heat down further and allow to gently simmer for about 30 minutes, again stirring regularly. Preheat the oven to 150°C/300°F/gas 2.

3 Taste it. Does it need more spice or sugar? Adjust if necessary. Ask your child to help you lightly grease a shallow ovenproof dish and pour in the rice pudding. Sprinkle a light dusting of ground nutmeg (or fresh, if you have it).

4 Place the rice pudding in the preheated oven for about 20 minutes, until a golden crust has formed. Allow to cool slightly before serving.

GOURMET FOR GROWN-UPS

I'd add the full ½ tsp of cinnamon and not miss out on the nutmeg here – plus I would perhaps add some stewed plums for a bit of extra flavour and texture – and perhaps the zest of an orange too? You could also add in some dried fruits.

SIMPLE ROASTED VEGETABLES WITH COUSCOUS

I had all kinds of ambitious plans to introduce kids to couscous (I have in the past cooked it with purple grape juice and crushed blueberries to create 'purple pancakes'). But a simple Sunday lunch over at our good friends Maddy and Russell's reminded me recently of the simplicity of couscous – and, more pertinently, the fact that it actually serves us better when it plays a supporting role rather than trying to be the main event. I love halloumi and think it adds a fun and unexpected dimension to the flavours. I serve a big dish of this with a plateful of sizzling sausages – and very little gets left to waste.

COOKERY SKILLS: I CAN COAT VEGETABLES IN OIL – WITH MY HANDS!

SHOPPING LIST

(Ensure all the veg and the halloumi are cut to the same size)

250 g (8 oz) squash, peeled and chopped

100 g (3½ oz) parsnip, peeled and chopped

350 g (11½ oz) new baby potatoes, quartered or halved

1 red onion, chopped

100 g (3½ oz) raw beetroot, peeled and chopped

2 red peppers, deseeded and chopped

4 garlic cloves, peeled but not chopped

A good pinch of sea salt

7 tbsp olive oil

150 g (5 oz) halloumi cheese, chopped

A few sprigs of fresh rosemary

125 g (4 oz) couscous

SERVES 6–8

APRONS ON, LET'S COOK!

1 Preheat oven to 220°C/425°F/ gas 7.

2 Place all of the vegetables, the garlic, salt and the olive oil in a big shallow baking or casserole dish.

3 With your hands, and your child's if they're willing, mix to combine it all, ensuring all the veg is coated in the oil. Add the chopped halloumi and the sprigs of rosemary.

4 Cook in the preheated oven for about 30 minutes. If you want to serve this with sausages, put some in the oven on a baking tray after the vegetables have been cooking for 10 minutes (or follow the guidelines on the pack) – do ensure they're cooked thoroughly.

5 After 20 minutes of the vegetables cooking, put the couscous in a bowl (or saucepan with lid) and pour over 150 ml (¼ pint) boiling water (or use a light vegetable stock) so it is just covered. Cover with cling film, a plate or the saucepan lid and leave for 5 minutes. Then use a fork to separate the grains, which will have soaked up all the liquid.

6 After 25 minutes of the veg cooking, take it out of the oven and stir in the couscous. Return the baking dish back to the oven for another 5 minutes so that the couscous absorbs some of the juice and flavour from the veg. If you wanted, you could also add in some (cooked) chopped sausages here too.

GOURMET FOR GROWN-UPS

I'm not quite sure that this dish needs 'poshing' up – although Matt loves it when I've bought some spicy sausages and chopped and stirred those through (once cooked). I do like to serve it with some artisan bread to mop up the juices. This is an incredibly simple dish.

beans and pulses

MARKETING BEANS & PULSES

Once again, art and craft activities do come into their own here. There has been many a time when my three would come home from playschool with a lovingly prepared piece of artwork incorporating glued-on dried beans and sea shells etc (to this day I have one on the wall in the bathroom). The more familiar your kids become with these funny-shaped and coloured foods, the less alien it will seem to cook with them, and therefore (in theory) the more open they'll be to trying them.

TRY THIS...

People are often put-off making their own hummus and I agree that it's so readily available in shops that to go down the DIY option may seem like a real faff. But the beauty of making hummus with kids is that you don't have to stick to exacting measurements and can adjust everything to taste. So why not spend some time with your child creating your own 'personal blend'? There are countless recipes online – or use my recipe on page 44 as a base from which to work.

BACON BUTTER BEAN MASH

So this is a bit of a marmite one – in my experience kids either love it or hate it – but it's worth a try. The bacon is optional – although I happen to think it goes really well with the butterbeans and ups the protein further. The ricotta is an essential part of this recipe – it adds depth of flavour and a lovely creaminess. The breadcrumb topping is simply to add a bit of texture and prettiness (butter beans alone, mashed, can look a bit odd to a child).

COOKERY SKILLS: I CAN PRACTISE MASHING

SHOPPING LIST

2 knobs of butter

25 g (1 oz) fresh breadcrumbs

1 x 400 g (13 oz) tin butter beans, drained and rinsed

50 ml (2 fl oz) hot light vegetable stock (use only half the quantity of stock cube or powder recommended)

½ tsp Dijon mustard

1–2 tbsp ricotta cheese

2 bacon rashers, cooked and chopped into pieces

SERVES 2–4

APRONS ON, LET'S COOK!

1 Melt a knob of butter in a small non-stick frying pan. Add the breadcrumbs and sauté over a medium heat for 3 minutes until warm and crispy. Set aside.

2 Get your child to help place the butter beans, stock, another knob of butter and the mustard in a saucepan. Heat up and as you do so, mash up the beans (an older child could also help to do this under supervision).

3 Add the ricotta and bacon and mix well. Serve immediately, topping each serving with some crispy breadcrumbs.

NOTE
I tend to trim all the fat off the bacon with kitchen scissors. You can adjust the amount of bacon if you like.

GOURMET FOR GROWN-UPS

I never muck about with this too much – except perhaps to add some sautéed garlic and onion, and occasionally a small squeeze of lemon juice. When I have served this to guests, I generally decant small amounts into oven proof ramekins, top with the breadcrumbs and a bit of grated parmesan and finish off under the grill, serving as a side to meat or fish.

GOURMET FOR GROWN-UPS

Essentially this is already a soup-ed up version of a classic so I wouldn't play much further. But friends have expressed audible delight when I've switched the regular potatoes to sweet potatoes and poshed up the cheese a bit.

FINN'S BAKED BEAN SHEPHERDS PIE – WITH A TWIST OF CABBAGE!

I was *this* close to adding something cool and virtuous to this recipe – mung beans for example. But I think good old fashioned baked (haricot) beans do the job just fine. In any case, the sweet chilli sauce is controversial enough as an ingredient here. This is one of those recipes that you can strip right back to its basics – and feel free to do just that – skip out on the sweet chilli sauce for starters if you feel it's a step too far; or lose the added vegetables in the mash – especially the cabbage if you think it will be a sticking point.

COOKERY SKILLS: I CAN PRACTISE PEELING AND MASHING POTATO

SHOPPING LIST

500 g (1 lb) minced lamb
1 small onion, finely diced
1 carrot, peeled and diced
1 x 400 g (14 oz) tin baked beans
250 ml (8 fl oz) hot stock of your choice
1–2 tbsp sweet chilli sauce (or to taste)
2 tbsp tomato purée
1 tbsp Worcestershire sauce (or to taste)
1 tbsp plain flour
50 g (2 oz) grated cheese

For the mash:
625 g (1¼ lb) potatoes, peeled and chopped
200 g (7 oz) root vegetables, eg parsnips, chopped
200 g (7 oz) shredded Savoy cabbage
25 g (1 oz) butter
50 ml (2 fl oz) whole milk
2 tbsp ricotta or cream cheese
Salt and pepper

SERVES 6

APRONS ON, LET'S COOK!

1 Start with the mash. Cover the potatoes in a large saucepan with boiled water (more than you need for just the spuds) and simmer for 10 minutes. Add the parsnips and continue on a rapid simmer for another 10 minutes. Add the cabbage and continue for a final 5 minutes. Drain everything then return to the pan with the butter, milk and ricotta cheese. Mash, mash, mash until smooth and creamy – a perfect job for your kids to help with. Season to taste and set aside.

2 Preheat the oven to 200°C/400°F/gas 6. Dry fry the mince with the onion over a medium heat in a non-stick frying pan for about 3 minutes, stirring to break it up a bit. You don't need to add any fat or oil as there's enough fat with the meat.

3 I now like to get rid of all or most of the fat that has come out of the mince, so (using a slotted spoon) I transfer all the meat to a large non-stick saucepan. Let the excess fat from the frying pan cool a bit then discard, pouring into the bin – not down the sink.

4 Add the carrots and flour and stir through for a minute or two to prevent any lumps forming. Add the baked beans, stock, chilli sauce, Worcestershire sauce and tomato purée to the mince. Let this gently simmer for 1–2 minutes to thicken, but keep stirring. Maybe older kids could help out with the stirring here under supervision.

5 Have a quick taste. Are you happy with it? Are the kids? Does it need anything else?

6 Transfer to a casserole dish, top with the mashed potato and ask a child to sprinkle over some cheese for the topping. Bake in the middle of the preheated oven for around 15 minutes, until golden and bubbly.

lentils and legumes

MARKETING LENTILS AND LEGUMES

I will simply refer you here to the 'beans and pulses' idea of getting your kids handling certain foods for this group – be it by means of an arts and crafts activity or by simply getting hands-on in the kitchen. Once again it's also worth pointing out to your kids how 'magical' certain foods can be when left to soak overnight – they 'drink up' the water and become softer.

TRY THIS...

Think about ways in which you can replace meat and fish with lentils. There are countless recipes online and (usually) in veggie cookbooks for lentil burgers for example. Perhaps thin the split pea soup out with a little more stock and use as a pasta sauce? Equally you could use less stock with the lentil pasta sauce and eat as a soup. Or how about serving either – thick and decanted into clean glass bottles – and introducing them as 'yellow' or 'red' ketchup that they can dip their chips into?

POWER-PACKED PASTA SAUCE

This is really easy to make, jam-packed with vitamins and is freezable too (if you fancy doubling the quantities and making a big batch). It includes five portions of vegetables along with a good dose of protein from the addition of red lentils. Don't skip out on the seasoning at the end – this enhances as well as pulls together all those flavours.

COOKERY SKILLS: I CAN PRACTISE MY CHOPPING SKILLS

SHOPPING LIST

2 tbsp olive oil

1 small onion, finely chopped

1 garlic clove, finely chopped

½ courgette (about 100 g (3½ oz), sliced and finely chopped

1 carrot, grated

1 red or orange pepper, deseeded and diced

1 x 400 g (13 oz) tin chopped tomatoes

1 tbsp tomato purée

500 ml (17 fl oz) light hot vegetable stock (1 tsp boullion to 500 ml (17 fl oz) boiled water)

100 g (3½ oz) red split lentils

1 generous tablespoon fresh basil leaves

A good pinch of salt and black pepper

1–2 tsp dark brown sugar

MAKES ABOUT 1 LITRE (1¾ PINTS) SAUCE

APRONS ON, LET'S COOK!

1 Heat the oil in a large non-stick saucepan. Add the onion and garlic and sauté, gently, for a minute or two.

2 Add the courgette, carrot and pepper and continue to cook for a minute. Don't you just love the smell of this? And looking at it, you just know its good for you too.

3 Add the chopped tomatoes and tomato purée and stir round. Pour in the stock and the lentils and give it all another big stir. Maybe an older child can stir too?

4 Bring to the boil then simmer gently for about 10–15 minutes, stirring occasionally (until the lentils have softened).

5 Take the saucepan off the heat, add the basil, seasoning and sugar and give it another good stir. Allow to cool slightly.

6 Transfer the sauce to a blender or food processor and whizz until smooth. Taste and adjust the seasoning if necessary. Serve with pasta shapes, top with grated cheese and maybe some more fresh basil too.

GOURMET FOR GROWN-UPS

Funnily enough, as I type I'm just eating a plateful of this sauce with a little pasta left over from the kids' tea! I cooked it as above, but first sautéed some extra onion, garlic, pine nuts and chopped red chillies in olive oil – then added a few ladles of the sauce and then the cooked pasta. Ok, hardly gourmet – but you wouldn't exactly serve such a chilli kick to kids either.

SUNNY SOUP

This is a real winter warmer. It also really plays on the senses – the smell of it all cooking; the sound of it bubbling away; the sight of the yellow and orange ingredients. Do play up to this when you add the vegetables 'look at the different kinds of orange! What's your favourite?'

Making your own soup is really simple – all you need is a bit of time to prepare the vegetables – which let's face it can be done the night before – and a blender or food processor. That said, this particular soup also uses split yellow peas which need pre-soaking – just put them in a bowl with some cold water, that's it. When chopping the carrot, squash and potato, try to keep them roughly the same sort of size – and not too small either.

COOKERY SKILLS: I CAN DRAIN AND RINSE SPLIT PEAS

SHOPPING LIST

100 g (3½ oz) split yellow peas, soaked overnight

1 tsp unsalted butter

1 tbsp olive oil

1 small onion, diced

1 litre (1¾ pints) good-quality hot vegetable stock

1 small sweet potato, roughly chopped

1 large carrot, roughly chopped

The thin end of a small butternut squash, peeled and chopped

SERVES 6

APRONS ON, LET'S COOK!

1 Drain the peas and ask a child to rinse them through with cold water. Set aside.

2 In a large saucepan, melt the butter and the oil. Saute the onion for a couple of minutes. Add all the vegetables and stir round for another minute or so – notice the smells and colours, as suggested above.

3 Add the split peas and pour over 800 ml (1¼ pints) of the hot stock. Stir and simmer rapidly for about 40 minutes, stirring occasionally.

4 Transfer to a blender or food processor and blitz until smooth. Transfer the soup back to the saucepan. Is it too thick for you or just right? Feel free to top up slightly (and stir through) with the stock you've held back.

5 Serve with crusty bread and enjoy.

NOTE
If this ends up as popular with your kids as it is mine, double the quantities and freeze a batch for next time.

GOURMET FOR GROWN-UPS

I love slicing lots of fresh garlic and adding to the pan with the onion. I sometimes add a chopped red chilli too. Serve with a dollop of crème fraîche or plain yogurt and garnish with fresh coriander.

going global

MARKETING GLOBAL FOODS

I think one of the nicest ways to introduce kids to international flavours and cuisine is to introduce your child to different cultures. Travelling to other countries is the most obvious (although costly) way of doing this. But you could also use specific TV shows (channels and shows dedicated to travel), grab a globe or atlas and take a look. Go online and see what you can find.

TRY THIS...

A friend once cooked up a fantastic fruity curry using banana rather than meat or fish – it went down a storm with a lot of kids and I now wish I'd pinched the recipe. There's no reason why you couldn't try making sushi with your kids either, ditching the fish if you think it will be a problem and instead use pretty, colourful vegetables.

PATIENT PIZZA

Ok, so what kid doesn't love pizza? You may well think that I was struggling for a second recipe idea here (loosely speaking, this is a nod to Italy – but pizza is now so mainstream in so many cultures that, granted, I'm on slightly shaky ground here). The truth is, I just really wanted to share this recipe with you – it's so good and so incredibly different to how pizza dough is normally made – plus it teaches patience. Let me state quickly that it is actually a recipe derived from Peter Reinhart – an American food writer and baker with a brilliant expertise on all-things dough-related. I should also stress that I've modified Peter's original recipe for the purposes of this book (he knows this); the real thing goes into far more exacting detail.

The dough, though very moist, is surprisingly easy to work with as long as you keep a bit of extra flour to hand. I know that precision in recipes – particularly with baking – can be nerve-racking, but just follow the recipe to the letter and you'll be fine. Phase 1 is about holding your nerve; phase 2 is simply time-management and staying on track with your measurements. A little note though: this is one for the food processor (assuming your's has a dough hook). Yes, you can do it by hand, but why make life harder.

As you'll see, this is a recipe for you as much as the kids. I'd get the kids involved at phase 1 and then later at the fun part – putting on the toppings.

SHOPPING LIST

575 g (1 lb 2 oz) strong white flour, such as '00' grade (if you're reading this ahead of time, chill the flour in the fridge), plus extra for dusting

1 tsp salt

1 tsp dried active yeast

5 tbsp olive oil, plus extra for oiling

400 ml (14 fl oz) very cold water (measure it out and put it in the freezer for 20–30 minutes)

Semolina, for dusting the bases

Pizza toppings of your choice

SERVES 6–8

APRONS ON, LET'S COOK!

PHASE 1:

1 Sift the flour and salt into the bowl of your food processor. Add the yeast, olive oil and cold water. With the dough hook on, set the speed to very low for 2 minutes. Go to a slighter faster speed for another 5 minutes. Look at the dough: it should look moist and sticky (don't panic!) – sticking to the bottom of the bowl – but not to the sides.

2 Generously oil six large sealable plastic freezer bags. Flour a surface with your hands. Tip the dough onto the surface and use your hands to encourage it out. Lightly flour the surface of the dough as you go.

3 Divide the dough into six even portions, rounded into a ball. Lift each portion into a plastic bag and resprinkle the top of each with a dusting of flour. Seal and place the bags into the fridge for anywhere between one and three days (yes, really!). These can also be placed in the freezer for up to 3 months. If you do this, then thaw them overnight in the refrigerator and then go from the next step. This part of your job is done.

PHASE 2:

4 About 5 hours before you want to bake the pizzas, take the bags out of the fridge and bring the dough to room temperature.

5 Once it's at room temperature, dust your hands with flour, flour your work surface and remove the dough from their bags, shaping into small discs of about 12 cm (5 in) diameter and about 1 cm (½ in) in thickness. Don't worry if some of the dough sticks to the bags. Lightly dust the discs with a little more flour and leave to rest for 2 hours, loosely covered with a couple of clean plastic bags.

6 Preheat a hot oven for at least 20–30 minutes before it's needed to 240°C/475°F/gas 9. If you have a pizza stone heat this up too – if not, use a baking tray (but don't preheat the baking tray).

7 Once the oven is getting hot, dust your baking tray with some semolina (or remove the pizza stone when ready to bake and dust that). If you're brave – and experienced – you can now shape your dough by hand (using the fist and spin method). I'm neither of the above and simply do the following: place a disc onto a lightly floured surface and ease it out to at least 23 cm (9 in). Lightly flour the dough and then carefully place it onto the hot stone (use a rolling pin to help you). If you're using a baking tray, simply do all your pressing out work on the tray.

8 Now to toppings – perhaps get the kids in to help here. The key to keeping this base intact is not to now go and ruin your work and dedication by adding on loads of toppings. Simply use a pasta-style tomato sauce as a base, some grated cheese (not loads and loads) and one or two other light toppings. If you over-load with toppings, it makes it harder for the dough to bake.

9 Bake in the preheated oven for around 6–7 minutes. Don't over-cook it.

NUTTY NOODLES

This is a little introductory dish to some of those gorgeous Thai flavours: lime, sesame, nuts and chilli. Of course there are other flavours in Thai cuisine too – but I've kept this version pretty laid-back. Please feel free to play about with it though. And if the sauce is too thick for your child's liking, loosen it further by adding a bit more hot water. You could cook this up for yourself – and see if your child fancies grazing from your plate (a tried and tested – if a little controversial – Toddler Chef method). Try using the sauce with cooked pasta too.

COOKERY SKILLS: I CAN LEARN HOW TO STIR-FRY

SHOPPING LIST

200 g (7 oz) cooked egg noodles (you may find it better to chop these up a bit)

100 g (3½ oz) stir-fry vegetables of your child's choice (optional at this stage)

For the nutty noodle sauce:

2 tbsp smooth, natural peanut butter

2 tbsp sweet chilli sauce

2 tbsp hot water from the kettle

2 tsp sesame oil

1 tsp soy sauce or tamari sauce

Juice of 1 lime

SERVES 2–4

APRONS ON, LET'S COOK!

1 Put all of the sauce ingredients into a small bowl and ask a child to whisk until smooth.

2 Place the sauce in a wok or non-stick frying pan with the cooked noodles (or pasta if you prefer) and stir to combine. Add any veg you want to use at this stage.

3 Stir-fry for a few minutes until everything's heated through.

NOTE
Always check for any nut allergies. Young babies should not be offered nuts.

GOURMET FOR GROWN-UPS

Try adding some chopped fresh ginger (your child may just like a little of this too). I love fresh coriander and would definitely add some to the finished dish – a good handful on the top. I'd also add a sprinkling of sesame seeds. In terms of vegetables, go for whatever you fancy – plus think about adding chicken, fish or seafood.

ABOUT THE AUTHOR

Writer, broadcaster, and children's cookery expert, Fiona is a woman on a mission: to get kids truly excited about good food, banishing 'fussy eating' forever! Neither a chef nor nutritionist, Fiona is simply a parent with a unique story to tell, having converted her own kids from 'fruit dodgers' and 'veggie avoiders' into fully-blown mini 'foodies'. While experiencing tantrums, tears and mealtime meltdowns, Fiona began to watch (and then study) how and why kids eat in the way that they do, and the effect we as parents have on their eating behaviours. She then went on to devise a set of recipes and techniques that totally transformed her families eating habits, inspiring her to jack in the day job and set up Toddler Chef – which operates classes and workshops for Under-5's.

Fiona now also works closely with schools and pre-schools, and children of all ages including 'tweens' and teens. On a corporate level she has consulted with and worked alongside a number of companies – including Waitrose Plc and various holiday companies. In 2010 Fiona was invited by Unilever to become their new Flora Mum, creating family-friendly and heart-healthy recipes via Facebook.

With a background in voice-over and radio presentation, she is frequently used by BBC Radio as a spokesperson on healthy eating for children and has also been hired as a speaker at a number of prestigious 'foodie' events –

including The Children's Food Festival in Oxfordshire (of which Raymond Blanc is a patron). Fiona continues to work as a freelance food and travel writer for a variety of newspapers and magazines, including *The Independent*, and is a regular columnist for Foodepedia, the online food and travel site.

Fiona lives in Somerset with her husband, son, two daughters and far too many bathroom products.

For further information on Fiona, her consultancy work, the workshops, franchises and product range go to www.toddlerchef.com as well as www.fionafaulkner.co.uk. You can also sign up at both of these sites for free quarterly newsletters – with exclusive recipes, offers, tips, and news.

Index

A

apples 72
  chicken and Parmesan secret
    sausages 99
  creamy rhubarb mocktail 73
  pink porridge 82
  Somerset eggs 105
aubergines 84
  aubergine crispies 86–7
avocados 56
  Elsie's avocado ice cream 57
  sushi sandwiches 58

B

bacon: bacon butter bean mash 113
  caramelized pear puffs with goats'
    cheese and bacon 97
baked bean shepherds pie 115
bananas: banana peanut butter
    smoothie 80
  butternut and banana smoothie 50
  strawberry and banana breakfast
    milkshake 81
  tropical clafoutis 77
beans 112, 116
bread 104
  pea and cranberry crostini 37
  scrambled egg cupcake stars 107
  sushi sandwiches 58
breakfast 80
broccoli 32
  baby broccoli pasta 33
  broccoli baked potatoes 34–5
butter bean mash 113
butternut squash *see* squash

C

cakes 43, 74
caramelized pear puffs 97
carrots 28
  orange spaghetti 30–1
  sunny soup 118

cauliflower 68
  cauliflower cheese mash 69
cereals, breakfast 80
champ, parsley 94
cheese: caramelized pear puffs with
    goats' cheese and bacon 97
  cauliflower cheese mash 69
  cheesy tomato crumble 25
  chicken and Parmesan secret
    sausages 99
  crispy leek and Cheddar muffins 66
  Emily's pea and lime dip 39
  Mediterranean mac and cheese 91
  mushroom and halloumi skewers 85
  red pepper pizzas 46–7
  savoury olive loaf 89
  simple roasted vegetables with
    couscous 110
  smoked salmon crispy pancakes
    101
  spinach, feta and cranberry parcels
    62
  spinach pesto 61
chicken and Parmesan secret
  sausages 99
chickpeas: hummus in a hurry 44
chips 65, 93
chowder, creamy corn 41
citrus fruits 72
clafoutis, tropical 77
coconut cream ice lollies 79
courgettes 68
  courgette and lime sorbet 71
couscous, simple roasted vegetables
  with 110
cranberries: pea and cranberry
    crostini 37
  spinach, feta and cranberry parcels
    62
crisps 52
crostini, pea and cranberry 37
crumble, cheesy tomato 25

D

Darcey's inside-out tomato
  sandwiches 26
deli foods 88
dips 39, 44
dried fruit 21

E

eggs 104
  scrambled egg cupcake stars 107
  Somerset eggs 105
Elsie's avocado ice cream 57
Emily's pea and lime dip 39
exotic fruit 76

F

Finn's baked bean shepherds pie 115
fish 100
Five Senses Game 64

G

global foods 120
golden brown rice pudding 109
green bean polenta chips 65
greens 64

H

herbs 92
hummus in a hurry 44

I

ice cream, Elsie's avocado 57
ice lollies, coconut cream 79

K

kiwi fruit 72
  kiwi and lime cupcakes 74

L

lamb: Finn's baked bean shepherds
  pie 115
leeks 64

crispy leek and Cheddar muffins 66
lentils and legumes 116

M
mac and cheese 91
meat 96
meatballs with a twist 102
Mediterranean mac and cheese 91
milk: golden brown rice pudding 109
   pink porridge 82
   strawberry and banana breakfast
    milkshake 81
muffins, crispy leek and Cheddar 66
mushrooms 84
   mushroom and halloumi skewers 85

N
noodles, nutty 123

O
oats: pink porridge 82
olive loaf, savoury 89

P
pancakes 55, 101
parsley champ 94
parsnips 28
   parsnip risotto 29
pasta: baby broccoli pasta 33
   Mediterranean mac and cheese 91
   orange spaghetti 30–1
   power-packed pasta sauce 117
pastries 62, 97
patient pizza 120-1
peanut butter smoothie 80
pear puffs, caramelized 97
peas 36
   Emily's pea and lime dip 39
   pea and cranberry crostini 37
pecans: sweet potato and pecan
   pancakes 55
peppers 44

hummus in a hurry 44
   red pepper pizzas 46–7
pesto: baby broccoli pasta 33
   spinach pesto 61
pine nuts: meatballs with a twist 102
   spinach pesto 61
pineapple: butternut and banana
   smoothie 50
   tropical clafoutis 77
pizzas 46–7, 120-1
polenta chips, green bean 65
porridge, pink 82
potatoes 52
   broccoli baked potatoes 34–5
   crisps 52
   Finn's baked bean shepherds pie
    115
   mushroom and halloumi skewers 85
   parsley champ 94
   potato pillows 53
power-packed pasta sauce 117
puff pastry 47
pumpkin 48

R
rhubarb 72
   creamy rhubarb mocktail 73
rice 108
   golden brown rice pudding 109
   parsnip risotto 29
risotto, parsnip 29

S
sausages: chicken and Parmesan
   secret sausages 99
   Somerset eggs 105
savoury olive loaf 89
scones, squashy 49
shepherds pie, Finn's baked bean 115
slimy foods 84
smoked salmon crispy pancakes 101
smoothies 50, 80

Somerset eggs 105
sorbet, courgette and lime 71
soups 41, 118
sour fruit 72
spaghetti, orange 30–1
spices 92
spinach 60
   spinach, feta and cranberry parcels
    62
   spinach pesto 61
split peas: sunny soup 118
spring onions: parsley champ 94
squash 48
   butternut and banana smoothie 50
   squashy scones 49
   sunny soup 118
strawberry and banana breakfast
   milkshake 81
sunny soup 118
sushi sandwiches 58
sweet potatoes: sunny soup 118
   sweet potato and pecan pancakes
    55
sweetcorn 40
   creamy corn chowder 41
   sweet spiced sunshine cakes 43

T
tomatoes 24–7
   cheesy tomato crumble 25
   Darcey's inside-out tomato
    sandwiches 26
   red pepper pizzas 46–7
tortilla chips, baked spiced 93
tropical clafoutis 77
tuna: meatballs with a twist 102

V
vegetables: nutty noodles 123
   power-packed pasta sauce 117
   simple roasted vegetables with
    couscous 110

Acknowledgements

First I'd like to raise a plastic tumbler of smoothie to everyone who's ever attended or supported one of my workshops or classes. Thank you also to the businesses that have supported me along the way – in particular Waitrose (especially the Buckingham and Milton Keynes branches).

Tony Collins Fogarty. Where do I begin?! Thanks for not only creating fantastic websites, video content and web support – but also for sound advice and a lot of laughs along the way. It's my pleasure to plug www.tdfmedia.co.uk.

Alison Foster! Big thanks for your belief in my project. You kick-started a lot of stuff for me (and gave my backside a much-needed kick as well!)

Borra Garson, Jan Croxson, and all at DML – big thanks, big hugs and big smiles! I love working with you guys and it's great to know I'm on your team.

Clare Sayer at New Holland. I'm just thrilled we've been able to work together and your enthusiasm for(and dedication to) this project has gone a long way. Thank you, thank you!

To anyone who's ever lent me their kitchen (as well as laughter and endless cups of tea) – particularly during one of our many house moves: James and Clare Gibson; the lovely and always encouraging Michelle and Justin Chadwick; Heather and Jason Brogden; Caroline and Andrew Hines (visit Gawcott's finest PYO!); Katie and Simon England (kitchen envy? me?); Jenny and Tim Beebee (hasn't your's been on stand-by at least twice?) …crikey, I've borrowed a lot of kitchens. (Oh and thanks to Sarah and Colin Plummer for creating a lovely new kitchen that was finally ours – only for us to go and move to Somerset…)

And to other friends who've just been a massive support generally while I've been working and writing ('can you look after the kids…again?'): Brenda Page (huge big hugs); Rachel Sleeman (she of the Little Black Book in the city); Maddie and Russell Mills (two of my favourite people in the world); and of course my NCT Gals: Andrea Pepper, who is just lovely, and Julie Tecko, who is one of the very best friends a girl could ever have. Ju, I owe you. x.

To everyone who's ever supported my writing – or, better still (!), *paid* me to write: Nick Harmen at Foodepedia; Kate Simon at The Independent; and everyone on the Flora Mum project – both at TMW and Unilever.

Thank you Mary Cadogan and Peter Reinhart for generously allowing me to borrow from one each of your recipes. Google both for more on their inspiring work.

To every chef I've ever admired (Stephanie Alexander; Nigel Slater; Jamie Oliver; Michael Caines; Hugh Fearnly-Whittingstall… the list is endless) and to my mum, who first instilled in me a fascination with cookery shows and recipe books – thank you. On that same note, thanks dad – for always encouraging me to write. Mary and Jeremy Rice: quite simply thank you for always being there.

Finally to my wonderful husband Matt who has always supported my mad ideas and crazy work schedule – and still found the time to do an amazing radio show as well as make Miss Fussy here a colour-chart-perfect cuppa every Saturday morning (some wives are high-maintenance with their shoes; I guess I'm high maintenance with my tea). In the time-honoured 'us' tradition of quoting movie scenes, I'm dedicating Scene 23 from *Juno* to you and to us. Thank you for loving me for exactly who I am – even when I have PMS and tramp-style hair - *and* for being my very own (cool, rather more sexy version of) Bleeker. Here's to us and to life. Where will the adventure take us next…? x